1991–1993 …mination Questions
…gested Solutions

…ean Commu… Law

LLB

University of London
External Examinations

HLT Publications

HLT PUBLICATIONS
200 Greyhound Road, London W14 9RY

ISBN 0 7510 0416 2

British Library Cataloguing-in-Publication.

A CIP Catalogue record for this book is available from the British Library.

Printed and bound in Great Britain.

CONTENTS

ACKNOWLEDGEMENT

The questions used are taken from past University of London LLB (External) Degree examination papers and our thanks are extended to the University of London for the kind permission which has been given to us to use and publish the questions.

Caveat:

The answers given are not approved or sanctioned by the University of London and are entirely our responsibility.

They are not intended as 'Model Answers', but rather as Suggested Solutions.

The answers have two fundamental purposes, namely:

1. To provide a detailed example of a suggested solution to examination questions, and
2. To assist students with their research into the subject and to further their understanding and appreciation of the subject of Laws.

Note:

Please note that the solutions in this book were written in the year of the examination for each paper. They were appropriate solutions at the time of preparation, but students must note that certain caselaw and statutes may subsequently have changed.

Editor's Note:

We publish the *Past Examination Questions – Suggested Solutions* series of books together with this series. However, for this subject we have insufficient papers for the *Past Examination Questions – Suggested Solutions* and therefore we are including an extra paper in this book.

INTRODUCTION

Why choose HLT publications

Holborn College has earned an International reputation over the past ten years for the outstanding quality of its teaching, Textbooks, Casebooks and Suggested Solutions to past examination papers set by the various examining bodies.

Our expertise is reflected in the outstanding results achieved by our students in the examinations conducted by the University of London, the Law Society, the Council of Legal Education and the Associated Examining Board.

The object of Suggested Solutions

The Suggested Solutions have been prepared by College lecturers experienced in teaching to this specific syllabus and are intended to be an example of a full answer to the problems posed by the examiner.

They are not 'model answers', for at this level there almost certainly is not just one answer to a problem, nor are the answers written to strict examination time limits.

The opportunity has been taken, where appropriate, to develop themes, suggest alternatives and set out additional material to an extent not possible by the examinee in the examination room.

We feel that in writing full opinion answers to the questions that we can assist you with your research into the subject and can further your understanding and appreciation of the law.

Notes on examination technique

Although the SUBSTANCE and SLANT of the answer changes according to the subject-matter of the question, the examining body and syllabus concerned, the TECHNIQUE of answering examination questions does not change.

You will not pass an examination if you do not know the substance of a course. You may pass if you do not know how to go about answering a question although this is doubtful. To do well and to guarantee success, however, it is necessary to learn the technique of answering problems properly. The following is a guide to acquiring that technique.

Time

All examinations permit only a limited time for papers to be completed. All papers require you to answer a certain number of questions in that time, and the questions, with some exceptions carry equal marks.

It follows from this that you should never spend a disproportionate amount of time on any question. When you have used up the amount of time allowed for any one question STOP and go on to the next question after an abrupt conclusion, if necessary. If you feel that you are running out of time, then complete your answer in note form. A useful way of ensuring that you do not over-run is to write down on a piece of scrap paper the time at which you should be starting each part of the paper. This can be done in the few minutes before the examination begins and it will help you to calm any nerves you may have.

Reading the question

It will not be often that you will be able to answer every question on an examination paper. Inevitably, there will be some areas in which you feel better prepared than others. You will prefer to answer the questions which deal with those areas, but you will never know how good the questions are unless you read the whole examination paper.

You should spend at least 10 MINUTES at the beginning of the examination reading the questions. Preferably, you should read them more than once. As you go through each question, make a brief note on the examination paper of any relevant cases and/or statutes that occur to you even if you think you may not answer that question: you may well be grateful for this note towards the end of the examination when you are tired and your memory begins to fail.

Re-reading the answers

Ideally, you should allow time to re-read your answers. This is rarely a pleasant process, but will ensure that you do not make any silly mistakes such as leaving out a 'not' when the negative is vital.

The structure of the answer

Almost all examination problems raise more than one legal issue that you are required to deal with. Your answer should include the following:

Identify the issues raised by the question

This is of crucial importance and gives shape to the whole answer. It indicates to the examiner that you appreciate what he is asking you about.

This is at least as important as actually answering the questions of law raised by that issue.

The issues should be identified in the first paragraph of the answer.

Deal with those issues one by one as they arise in the course of the problem

This, of course, is the substance of the answer and where study and revision pays off.

If the answer to an issue turns on a provision of a statute, CITE that provision briefly, but do not quote it from any statute you may be permitted to bring into the examination hall.

Having cited the provision, show how it is relevant to the question.

If there is no statute, or the meaning of the statute has been interpreted by the courts, CITE the relevant cases

'Citing cases' does not mean writing down the nature of every case that happens to deal with the general topic with which you are concerned and then detailing all the facts you can think of.

You should cite only the most relevant cases – there may perhaps only be one. No more facts should be stated than are absolutely essential to establish the relevance of the case. If there is a relevant case, but you cannot remember its name, it is sufficient to refer to it as 'one decided case'.

Whenever a statute or case is cited, the title of statute or the name of the case should be underlined

This makes the examiner's job much easier because he can see at a glance whether the relevant material has been dealt with, and it will make him more disposed in your favour.

Having dealt with the relevant issues, summarise your conclusions in such a way that you answer the question

A question will often say at the end simply 'Advise A', or B, or C, etc. The advice will usually turn on the individual answers to a number of issues. The point made here is that the final paragraph should pull those individual answers together and actually give the advice required. For example, it may begin something like: 'The effect of the answer to the issues raised by this question is that one's advice to A is that ...'

Related to the previous paragraph, make sure at the end that you have answered the question

For example, if the question says 'Advise A', make sure that is what your answer does. If you are required to advise more than one party, make sure that you have dealt with all the parties that you are required to and no more.

Some general points

You should always try to get the examiner on your side. One method has already been mentioned – the underlining of case names, etc. There are also other ways as well.

Always write as neatly as you can. This is more easily done with ink than with a ball-point.

Avoid the use of violently coloured ink eg turquoise; this makes a paper difficult to read.

Space out your answers sensibly: leave a line between paragraphs. You can always get more paper. At the same time, try not to use so much paper that your answer book looks too formidable to mark. This is a question of personal judgment.

NEVER put in irrelevant material simply to show that you are clever. Irrelevance is not a virtue and time spent on it is time lost for other, relevant, answers.

UNIVERSITY OF LONDON
LLB EXAMINATION 1990
PARTS I and II
for External Students

EEC LAW

Friday, 15 June: 10.00 am to 1.00 pm

Answer *FOUR* of the following EIGHT questions

1 Discuss the effect of the Single European Act on the influence of the European Parliament on law making in the Communities.

2 Okeefenokee plc, a subsidiary of a Dutch food company, distributes mineral water and other non-alcoholic drinks in the United Kingdom. Its current stock of products for sale and delivery includes a new drink called Swamp, which is described on the label as 'mineral water' but which consists in fact of carbonated tap water When visiting her local hypermarket a local authority officer notices the new product. On reading the label, she forms the view that the product contravenes a prohibition contained in a ministerial order on the stocking for sale and human consumption of products which are 'of defective composition'. This expression is not defined in the order. The officer considers, however, that in taking legal action against Okeefenokee she can rely on EC Council Directive 80/777. This Directive concerns the approximation of the laws of the Member States regarding the exploitation and marketing of natural mineral waters. It obliges Member States to ensure that only waters which meet certain requirements are marketed as natural mineral waters. Swamp does not satisfy these requirements. The deadline for giving effect to the Directive has not expired, and the United Kingdom has still not introduced implementing legislation. Learning of the possibility of legal action against it, Okeefenokee consults you regarding its position under European Community law.

Advise Okeefenokee.

3 Should the European Court of Justice ever refuse a national court's request for a preliminary ruling?

4 Liquidgold plc is one of only four manufacturers in the European Community of a new type of liquid sweetener manufactured from barley. Drinkitdown Ltd, a manufacturer of soft drinks, was so attracted by the economics of using this type of sweetener that it has installed new machinery in its factory suitable only for use with the barley sweetener. In January it entered into a contract with Liquidgold to purchase 10,000 tonnes of the sweetener each year for the next five years, this quantity being the amount needed to meet its current production requirements.

Last month, fearing adverse effects on the Community sugar industry, the Council adopted a regulation imposing production quotas on the barley sweetener. An annex to that regulation, which expressly refers to the four manufacturers by name, fixed Liquidgold's annual quota at 7,500 tonnes.

Having discovered that the other three manufacturers are already bound by contracts covering the whole of their permitted production, Drinkitdown is faced with a choice between cutting back its production or converting its factory to use sugar at a cost of £500,000.

Advise Drinkitdown as to the remedies available to it with regard to the Council Regulation.

5 Analyse TWO of the following decisions of the European Court of Justice and explain their importance in the development of Community law in the areas to which they relate:

a) Case 41/74 *Van Duyn* v *Home Office*

b) Case 8/74 *Dassonville*

c) Case 56 and 58/64 *Consten and Grundig*

d) Case 80/70 *Defrenne (No 1)*

6 ABC Ltd is the major French producer of goat cheese. It sends a shipment of cheese to a distributor in the United Kingdom, but the shipment is refused entry at the port of Dover. The reasons given by the Customs Inspector for refusing entry are, first, that the cheese is not labelled in English; secondly, that it is packed in cubic containers and therefore does not satisfy United Kingdom standards of consumer protection; and, thirdly, that it contains additives which are not allowed in cheese marketed in the United Kingdom.

Advise ABC Ltd as to its rights, if any, under European Community law.

7. British Breweries plc is an important producer of beer in the United Kingdom. Statistics show that British Breweries account for some 12 per cent of all beer sold in the United Kingdom but that its British Brewlite is especially successful and accounts for 40 per cent of all non-alcoholic beer consumed in the UK.

   a) British Breweries has been negotiating with County Beers Ltd with a view to merger. County Beers is the principal other producer of non-alcoholic beer and after merger the new company, British County Breweries, will control 65 per cent of the market in non-alcoholic beer.

   b) British Breweries includes in its standard supply contract a requirement that pubs and other purchasers must display prominently its non-alcoholic beer and advertising materials. The advertising materials offer consumers 'healthy drinking discounts' whereby the more non-alcoholic beer they buy, the lower price they have to pay. Since the healthy drinking discounts were introduced two years ago, British Breweries' sales have doubled and several small-scale producers of non-alcoholic beer have gone out of business.

   c) British Breweries want to establish a German subsidiary but have been advised that most retailers in Germany have agreed to purchase non-alcoholic beer only from the German Brewers' Association. The Association checks the quality of its members' products. However, there is a two-year trading requirement in Germany before a new brewery can be admitted to the Association.

   Advise British Breweries as to the significance, if any, of EEC law for each of the above aspects of its business.

8 To what extent is it true to say that once a person is qualified to practise law in one European Community country, he or she may practise law in any other European Community country?

QUESTION 1

General Comment

This is a straightforward but rather uninspired question concerning the changes introduced by the SEA to the position of the European Parliament in the law-making process. This question does not ask for a full analysis of the European Parliament's position in the Community.

Skeleton Solution

1 Brief outline of the position of the European Parliament before the SEA was enacted.

2 Changes introduced by the SEA with respect to the European Parliament's influence on law making.

3 Conclusion, including an assessment of the impact of the SEA on the European Parliament's position.

Suggested Solution

1 As a result of the EEC and Euratom Treaties and an inter-institutional agreement between the Parliament and the Council (1) the European Parliament has a right to be consulted on proposed legislation. The proposal is first considered by one of the Parliament's committees, which produces a report and a draft resolution. These go to the full Parliament which will give its opinion and may suggest amendments.

The Commission may modify its proposal on the basis of the Parliament's opinion but there is no obligation on either it or the Council to follow the opinion or to give reasons for rejecting it.

Although the European Parliament has no power to affect the content of legislation, its right to be consulted has received the support of the European Court of Justice in the case of *Roquette* v *Council* (2). This right 'implies that the Parliament has expressed its opinion. It is impossible to take the view that the requirement is satisfied by the Council's simply asking for the opinion'. If, however, any proposal is subsequently amended by the Council or the Commission the Court has held that there is no need for a second consultation with the Parliament if the provisions of the final text of the measure are 'substantially identical to those in the version submitted to the European Parliament' (3).

2 Despite the ruling in Roquette, the paucity of the European Parliament's power of influence in the legislation process is quite remarkable when compared to the powers held by parliaments in the member states and the European Council and Commission in the Community. These powers, however, were increased by articles 6 and 7 of the SEA which provide for a 'cooperation procedure', applicable only in certain circumstances, in which the EEC Treaty requires the Parliament to be consulted. This procedure, which is laid down in article 149(2) EEC (as amended by article 7 SEA), proceeds in the usual way as outlined above until the point is reached at which the Council would normally be ready to adopt the act. Instead of doing so, it merely adopts a 'common position', acting by a qualified majority, which is then sent to the Parliament, together with a statement of the reasons which led the Council to adopt the position and a statement of the Commission's position, for a second consideration. The Parliament has three months, with a possible one month extension by agreement, in which to approve or reject the common position, or to propose amendments to it. If the European Parliament approves the common position, or fails to take any action by the deadline, the Council will follow the common position.

If the European Parliament rejects the common position, the Council can adopt the act only by unanimity. This represents a real, although small, increase in the European Parliament's powers. Where the cooperation procedure applies, the measure can be blocked by an alliance between one member state and the Parliament. Being based on the Treaties, this new veto cannot be overridden by the other member states (the Luxembourg Accords now falling into abeyance).

If the European Parliament proposes amendments to the common position, the Commission must re-examine its proposal in the light of these amendments. It may adopt some or all of the Parliament's amendments but it is not obliged to do so. It then sends the proposal to the Council, enclosing the Parliament's amendments and a statement of reasons for rejecting them if the Commission decides not to incorporate any of the European Parliament's amendments into its proposal. The council can either accept the proposal as amended by the Commission, for which a qualified majority is sufficient, or it can amend the proposal, either by adopting amendments proposed by the Parliament or by adopting its own amendments. In these circumstances it can act only by unanimity. This does not represent a significant increase in the Parliament's powers. If the amendment is adopted by the Commission the Council can only reject it on a unanimous vote. This has always been the case. Furthermore, the Commission has always had the power to amend its proposal so as to give effect to amendments proposed by Parliament. All the new procedure does is to impose a legal obligation on the Commission to consider the Parliament's proposals, which it had always done in the past as a matter of practice, and to give reasons if it rejects it – hardly a substantial increase in the European Parliament's powers.

3 The cooperation procedure was adopted because of widespread dissatisfaction with the lack of democracy in the Community. The European Parliament, the only democratically elected institution, is also the weakest and the least influential of the law making bodies. The European Parliament was not happy with the cooperation procedure: it thought that its powers should be greater, and that the SEA did little to redress the balance of powers between the institutions. The above analysis appears to support this view. The SEA appears to grant the European Parliament little more than formal recognition by the member states of its status as a Parliament (rather than just an assembly) (4), without giving it the substantive powers to enable it to fulfil this role. Its greatest powers relate not to the influence it exerts over the law-making process but rather its power to make amendments to non-compulsory expenditure in the budget.

References

(1) European Parliament Resolution 65 of 27 November 1959
(2) *Roquette* v *Council*, Case 138/79 [1980] ECR 3333
(3) *Chemiefarma* v *Commission*, Case 41/69 [1970] ECR 661, paras 68 and 69
(4) Article 3(1) SEA 1986

QUESTION 2

General Comment

An interesting question, but don't be fooled into thinking it is a straight-forward question on the direct effect of directives.

Skeleton Solution

1 The similarity of this case to *Kolpinghuis*.

2 Can the local authority rely on the directive although it has not yet been implemented? – the law on direct effect?

3 Can the directive be used as an aid to interpretation of:

a) the attitude of the European court;

b) the attitude of the British courts?

Suggested Solution

1 A recent reference from Britain to the European Court addressed several of the issues raised by this question in a case where the facts were remarkably similar to those at issue here. In that case, *Officier van Justitie* v *Kolpinghuis Nijmegen* (1), criminal proceedings were brought against an undertaking running a cafe for stocking for sale and delivery a drink which it called 'mineral water' but which actually consisted of tap water and carbon dioxide. The undertaking was charged with infringing a national regulation which prohibited the sale of goods of unsound composition. The public prosecutor relied, inter alia, on Directive 80/777. The relevant provision of the Directive should have been implemented within four years after the Directive was notified, but the Dutch legislation was only amended five years after notification. The offences occurred before the Directive was amended.

2 According to the case law of the European Court, and in particular *Becker* (2), wherever the provisions of a directive appear to be unconditional and sufficiently precise, those provisions may be relied upon by an individual against the state (a term which is now broadly defined after *Foster*), where the state fails to implement the directive in national law by the end

of the prescribed period (*Ratti* (3)), for a state cannot plead, as against individuals, its own failure to perform the obligations which the directive entails. *Marshall* (4) made clear that a directive, being addressed to a member state, could not impose obligations on an individual and that a provision of a directive could not be relied upon against an individual. The Court therefore concluded in Kolpinghuis, and the same would apply in the case before us, that a national authority could not rely, as against an individual, upon a provision of a directive whose necessary implementation in national law had not yet taken place.

3 a) The next question, therefore, is whether the directive can be used as an aid to interpretation. In *Von Colson* (5), the European Court said 'that national courts when applying their domestic law, and in particular national legislation which had been specifically enacted to implement a directive, had a duty to interpret it in accordance with the wording and the purpose of the directive.'

Kolpinghuis, however, said that the application of the *Von Colson* principle was limited by the general principles of Community law and in particular the principles of legal certainty and non-retroactivity. The Court had ruled in *Pretore di Salo* v X (6) that a directive cannot of itself and independently of national law have the effect of determining or aggravating the liability in criminal law of people who act in contravention of the provisions of the directive. This was approved and applied *Kolpinghuis*. This provides Okeefenokee with strong grounds to argue that the unimplemented directive should not be used against it.

b) The English courts, however, have been prepared to adopt on occasion an adventurous approach to the interpretation of Community law provisions. In *ex p Schaffter*, Schiemann J gave a generous interpretation to the provisions of the Equal Treatment Directive. In *Pickstone* (7) and in *Litster* (8), the House of Lords, relying on s2(4) ECA 1972, amended by judicial fiat, the unambiguous words of the British legislation.

Anthony Arnull, a leading commentator in this field, points out that where the relevant rule of Community law is not directly effective, as is the case with Directive 80/777, the courts have been considerably less adventurous. Two cases illustrate this point – *Duke* v *GEC Reliance* (9) and *Finnegan* v *Clowney Youth Training Programme* (10). Both cases concerned the application of the Equal Treatment Directive to the Sex Discrimination Act (SDA) 1975 in the case of private employers. Since *Marshall* had confirmed that directives could only be applied vertically, this was an attempt to introduce horizontal direct effect. In the case of *Duke* the House of Lords argued that since the SDA was not introduced to implement the Equal Treatment Directive (whose deadline had already expired) there was no obligation to construe the national statute in line with the European legislation.

In *Finnegan*, the House of Lords confirmed this view, even though in that case the legislation which enacted the SDA in Northern Ireland, the Sex Discrimination (NI) Order 1976, did not come into force until after the Directive had been published. The Court argued that it would be inconsistent for the same legislation to have a different effect within different parts of the United Kingdom. This is despite the European Court's statement in *Johnston* (11) that the 1976 Order was to be interpreted in the light of the 1976 Directive.

On this evidence, it would seem that any British court would not be receptive to using the non-directly effective directive to interpret the ministerial order. Okeefenokee would therefore only have to defend its activities under national law.

References

(1) Case 80/86 [1989] 2 CMLR 18
(2) Case 30/66 [1967] ECR 285
(3) *Ratti*, Case 148/78 [1979] ECR 1629
(4) Case 152/84 [1986] 1 CMLR 688
(5) Case 14/83 [1984] ECR 1891
(6) Case 14/86 The Times, 20 June 1987
(7) *Pickstone* v *Freemans* [1988] 2 All ER 803
(8) [1989] 2 WLR 634
(9) [1988] 2 WLR 359
(10) [1990] IRLR 299
(11) [1989] ICR 83

See also: A Arnull, 'The Incoming Tide: Responding to Marshall' [1987] Public Law 383

Hepple and Byre, 'EEC Labour Law in the UK – a new approach' [1989] ILJ 129

QUESTION 3

General Comment

This is an interesting question but does require some knowledge of academic articles written on this subject. The answer below is by no means definitive and contains a very personal point of view.

Skeleton Solution

1 Introduction
2 The Treaty law
3 The European Court's policy
4 The problems which arise
5 *Foglia* v *Novello (Nos 1 and 2)* – the caselaw
6 Should the Court refuse a reference generally?
7 Are there circumstances where the Court should refuse a reference?
8 Conclusion.

Key Articles

Barav, 'Preliminary Censorship? The judgment of the European Court in *Foglia* v *Novello*' (1980) 5 EL Rev 443
Bebr, 'The Possible Implications of *Foglia* v *Novello II*' (1982) 9 CML Rev 421

Suggested Solution

1 For a long time, the European Court was very liberal in admitting references made by national courts pursuant to article 177 EEC. It admitted them, so it seemed, without any particular, formal examination of their admissibility.

2 Furthermore, while article 177 para 2 permits any Court or tribunal to refer a question of Community law to the European Court if it considers that a decision on the question is necessary to enable it to give judgment, article 177 para 3 obliges a court of last instance to refer such a question.

3 The European Court has always been anxious to admit references in order to have an opportunity to interpret Community law (*Hagen OHG* (Case 49/71)) and so develop the Community legal order. More importantly, encouraging national courts to make references served the dual purpose of both ensuring uniform interpretation of Community law, and familiarising the national courts with the existence of community law.

The success of this process, however, depended on the cooperation of the national courts. In order to sweeten the bitter pill of the supremacy of Community law over national law, the European Court has always emphasised the importance of this cooperative approach, rather than insisting on the development of a hierarchical structure which placed the European Court above the national courts, and claimed that there was a careful delimitation of responsibilities between the two courts, with the European Court interpreting Community law and the national courts applying this interpretation to the facts.

A careful balance, therefore, had to be struck by the European Court between furthering the aims of the internal market by ensuring the successful development of the Community legal order, and consideration for the sensitivities of the national system.

4 The popularity of this procedure and the growing awareness of the national Courts about the existence of a body of Community law has meant that the ECJ has started to become a victim of its own success. The sheer volume of references from the national courts has meant that no decision is given for up to two years in a particular case. Such a heavy workload means that the quality of the individual judgments may decrease and the quantity of judgments risks diluting their importance.

5 Yet in the leading case where the Court declined jurisdiction, *Foglia* v *Novello* (1), the European Court did not specifically address these problems. The case turned on its particular facts.

In *Foglia* v *Novello* a reference was made by an Italian court in an action between two Italians who had entered into a contract of sale requiring delivery of the goods in France. The contract provided that the buyer would not be responsible for the payment of any taxes imposed in contravention of Community law. The goods were duly delivered. The seller was required to pay a consumption tax in France and claimed reimbursement from the buyer, who refused to pay on the ground that the tax was contrary to Community law. Thus the Italian courts were required to decide whether the French tax was in accordance with Community law. This offended the European Court, for it entailed a challenge to the sovereign rights of another member state in a context where the state was not in a position to defend itself.

More importantly, there were grounds for believing that the whole transaction was contrived in order to raise a test case. For this reason, the European Court refused to accept the reference, stating that there was no genuine dispute between the parties. The Italian court was unwilling to accept this and made a second reference but the European Court remained adamant (2).

6 This ruling received a considerable amount of academic criticism, not least because it interfered with the delicate relationship between the national and European Courts. By imposing a requirement of a 'real dispute' between the parties as distinguished from, a 'question on matters of Community law' (thus cutting down on the number of potential references) this necessarily implies a review by the European Court of the national court's decision to refer, the reasons for the reference and the relevance of the question referred. This breaks down the cooperative framework and replaces it with a more hierarchical structure. Furthermore it obliges the European Court to investigate the facts of the case and to attempt to discover the real intention of the parties, thus trespassing on the national court's role as a fact finder.

7 Logic would suggest, however, that there are circumstances where the Court should, and indeed has, refused a reference. The first case is where the matter referred has no connection with Community law – see Cases 105/79, 68/80 and *Adlerblum*. The second case is where the requirements of article 177 are not satisfied – the reference is not made by a court or tribunal or the questions do not concern the interpretation of Community law or the validity of a Community Act. The third case is where the reference is an abuse of the procedure – an amorphous heading. In *Matthews* (3) the Court refused jurisdiction when it decided that the questions referred were purely hypothetical and that the parties had attempted to compel the national court to make a reference, thus depriving it of its discretion under the second paragraph of article 177. In *Foglia* v *Novello* it can be argued that jurisdiction was refused because the article 177 procedure was being abused by being employed to indirectly challenge a French tax when an article 169 proceedings would be more appropriate.

It could also be argued that fictitious litigation is an abuse of procedure, since mere academic consultation on a hypothetical issue is not the purpose of article 177. It is, however, difficult to develop reliable criteria for determining the existence of fictitious litigation – see *Chemical Farmaceutici* v *DAF* (4). Usually the Court has glossed over this requirement – see *Benedetti* v *Munari* (5), *Union Laitiere Normande* (6) and *Capolongo* v *Maya* (7).

8 In between the two rulings in *Foglia*, two other references were made to the European Court by courts in Italy: *Chemical* v *DAF* and *Vinal* v *Orbat* (8). Both cases had facts similar to those in Foglia, except the disputed tax was Italian and not French and the disputes were considered 'not to be manifestly bogus'. In both cases the European Court accepted the reference. It seems likely that the European Court's real reason for its decision in *Foglia* was one of policy – not to offend France.

The hostile reception received by Foglia and the potentially devastating consequences of the ruling on intra-judicial relationships may mean that the European Court has fought shy of extending such 'censorship' any further. It had, however, attempted to reduce its workload by using another tactic – the development of the acte clair doctrine after *CILFIT* (9) (although this is disputed by Rasmussen (1984) 9 EL Rev 242) which builds on rather than dismantles Euro-national judicial cooperation.

References

(1) Case 104/79 [1980] ECR 745
(2) Case 244/80 [1981] ECR 1
(3) Case 93/78 [1978] ECR 2203
(4) Case 140/79 [1981] ECR 1
(5) Case 52/76 [1977] ECR 163
(6) Case 244/78 [1979] ECR 2662
(7) Case 77/72 [1973] ECR 611
(8) Case 46/80 [1981] ECR 77
(9) Case 283/81 [1982] ECR 3415

QUESTION 4

General Comment

This question raises many issues relating to the article 173 judicial review procedure and requires a thorough knowledge of the substantive law relating to the locus standi requirements.

Skeleton Solution

1 Does the ECJ have jurisdiction:
   a) *ratione materiae*, ie is the act a reviewable act;
   b) is the act an act of the Council or the Commission;
   c) have the proceedings been instituted within the two month period?

2 Does the applicant have locus standi:
   a) as a privileged applicant; or
   b) as a non-privileged applicant;
      i) is the applicant a natural or legal person;
      ii) is the act a decision addressed to that person, a decision in the form of a regulation, or a decision addressed to another person;
      iii) and in the last two cases, is the decision of direct and individual concern to the applicant?

3 What are the grounds for review?

4 What are the consequences of the judicial review procedure?

5 Are there alternative methods of challenge?

Suggested Solution

1 Provided Drinkitdown institutes an action for article 173 proceedings within two months of the publication of the regulation or of its notification to the plaintiff (article 173(3)) the European Court will have jurisdiction to hear the matter. This is for two reasons; firstly a regulation is an 'act of the Council' and secondly a regulation is a reviewable act because, according to article 189, it has legal effects. (See further *Noordwijks Cement Accord Case* (1).)

2 b) i) Drinkitdown Ltd, a company and therefore a legal person, is a non-privileged applicant. To satisfy the locus standi requirements it needs to prove first that the Council regulation is in substance a decision and second that it is of direct and individual concern to Drinkitdown, so that Drinkitdown is a *de facto* addressee of the measure.

ii) The jurisprudence of the Court has concentrated on distinguishing decisions from regulations. The court has held, however, that the form of the legal act is not conclusive. By relying on article 189 it can be said that a decision is binding only on its addressee (actual or de facto) whereas a regulation is binding generally. This was the basis of the distinction used by the European Court in *Confederation Nationale* (2), the first major case in this area:

> 'The essential characteristics of a decision arise from the limitation of the persons to whom it is addressed, whereas a regulation, being essentially of a legislative nature, is applicable not to a limited number of persons, defined or identifiable, but to categories of persons viewed abstractly and in their entirety. Consequently, in order to determine in doubtful cases where one is concerned with a decision or a regulation, it is necessary to ascertain whether the measure in question is of individual concern to specific individuals.'

This test for distinguishing a decision from a regulation is very similar to the test for establishing individual concern, as set out by the Court in *Plaumann*, which is:

> 'Persons other than those to whom a decision is addressed may only claim to be individually concerned if that decision affects them by reason of certain attributes which are peculiar to them or by reason of circumstances in which they are differentiated from all other persons and by virtue of these factors distinguishes them individually, just as in the case of the person addressed' (3).

In later cases, however, a difference has emerged between the two tests. The first test, the test for deciding whether an act is a regulation or a decision, is based on the terms in which it is expressed. If it applies to abstractly defined categories of persons, it is a true regulation; if it applies only to named, or individually identified, individuals it is a decision. The second test, the test for individual concern is more generous and focuses on the persons whose legal rights are affected by the measure. The question to consider is whether they are affected as members of an open category, in which case they are not individually affected, or a closed category, in which case they are individually affected. It is quite possible for the second test to be satisfied while the first is not.

Unfortunately for Drinkitdown its case falls into an area where the Council legislates on policy matters using its discretion. The Court tends to impose stricter locus standi requirements in this area than it does in its quasi-judicial determinations in such areas as competition proceedings. (See Rasmussen, 'Why is article 173 interpreted against private plaintiffs' (1980) 5 EL Rev 112.) Moreover where the act is in the form of a regulation the Court has traditionally applied the first test first (whereas in the other cases it skips the first test and applies the second test), and has almost invariably found that the measure is in substance a regulation and the application is then declared inadmissible on locus standi grounds. See *Compagnie Francaise Commerciale* v *Commission* (4). In that case most of the provisions of the regulation at issue applied to an open category of persons but one provision applied to a closed category. The Court held that the measure was a true regulation which could not be challenged by a private applicant.

In *International Fruit Company* v *Commission* (5), however, the challenged measures concerned only a closed category of persons and the European Court held that the application was admissible. In *CAM* v *Commission* (6), a case whose facts were almost indistinguishable from *Compagnie Francaise*, the Court decided to consider the question of individual concern first, and by applying the closed category test and finding it satisfied, held that the application was admissible. There was no express finding that the measure was a decision. The same approach was adopted in *Exportation des Jucres* (7) and in *UNICME* v *Council*.

In subsequent cases, however, the Court swung back to the approach it adopted in *Compagnie Francaise*. The first case was *Beauport* v *Council and Commission*, a case where the entire regulation applied to a closed category, but the Court ruled that it was nevertheless a true regulation. Later cases decided on the same lines include *Wagner* v *Commission*, *Calpah*, *Moksel* and *Deutz*.

Most recently, in *Sofrimport Sarl* v *Commission* (8), however, the Court held that where a regulation applied to a closed category, an applicant was directly and individually concerned.

Other recent cases where the Court has allowed a private applicant to challenge an act in the form of a regulation have been *Agricola Commerciale Olio* v *Commission*, where the Court adopted a more liberal approach, *Salerno* v *Commission and Council*, a staff case, and *Roquette* v *Council*, whose facts closely resembled the ones at issue here. The measure concerned a closed category of persons, isoglucose producers who had previously been awarded a quota. The regulation included an annexe which listed the producers by name and stated exactly what their quotas would be under the new rules. The Court held that their application was admissible since the producers were directly and individually concerned by the regulation.

iii) After *Roquette*, Drinkitdown would have strong grounds to argue that it had locus standi for three reasons: firstly the regulation applied to named individuals and was therefore in substance a decision; secondly that Drinkitdown was individually concerned by virtue of its membership of a closed category. Although the category is theoretically open (and this may count against Drinkitdown – see *KSH* v *Council and Commission*) practically speaking it is closed because no new soft drink manufacturer may enter the market because the whole of the permitted production has been allocated. Thirdly the regulation affected Drinkitdown directly because as a result it was 2,500 tonnes short of the barley sweetener and would consequently have to cut back on its production or convert its factory to sugar. It may risk being refused locus standi, however, if the Court considers there is an alternative remedy open to it (see *Alusuisse* (9), *Spijker* (10) for example) or there is an alternative applicant who would have an interest in challenging the measure – Liquidgold for example.

3 The most likely ground for review is the infringement of the Treaty, or of 'any rule relating to its application'. This is a particularly wide ground of review and embraces Community acts as well as general principles of law.

4 If this plea is successful the Court can declare the regulation void. By article 174(2) the Court can state which of the effects of the regulation are definitive.

5 An alternative method of challenge is for Drinkitdown to bring an article 215(2) action in tort against the Council. Unlike the judicial review procedure there are no restrictions on the persons who may sue but Drinkitdown must bring an action within five years of the publication of the regulation.

The regulation is clearly an act imputable to the Community and Drinkitdown suffered damage as a result of its implementation. The European Court is willing to grant compensation to firms for financial losses – *Kampffmeyer* v *Commission* (11) and *CNTA* v *Commission* (12).

Special considerations apply where the alleged wrongful act on the part of the Community is an act intended to have legal effects. In *Plaumann* (13) the European Court ruled that a reviewable act which has not been quashed cannot form the basis of an action in tort. This was contrary to the Court's earlier ruling, brought under the ECSC Treaty, *Vloeberghs* v *High Authority* (14), where the Court emphasised that actions for damages and applications for review are quite separate proceedings. The later case of *Lütticke* v *Commission* (15), however, confirmed the Vloeberghs approach and admitted a tort action in a case where a reviewable act had not been quashed.

Schoppenstedt (16) confirmed the *Lütticke* approach and set out the principles governing Community liability for a normative act:

> '... the community does not incur liability on account of a legislative measure involving choices of economic policy unless a sufficiently serious breach of a superior rule of law for the protection of the individual has been breached'.

If the Council regulation is a true regulation this formula will apply to it. If the Council regulation is a disguised decision the formula will not apply but the formula's criteria will be taken into account in any consideration of the Council's liability.

While it is relatively easy for Drinkitdown to establish a breach of a superior rule of law ie any rule of Community law which would constitute a ground of annulment under article 173, it will be considerably harder for it to establish the breach 'manifestly and gravely disregarded the limits on the exercise of its powers' (the second *Skimmed Milk Powder* (17) case). It is unlikely that Drinkitdown will be able to satisfy this and thus its action will fail.

The other alternative remedy for Drinkitdown is to challenge the regulation indirectly by means of an indirect challenge. Under article 184 it is possible to challenge the validity of a regulation in the course of other proceedings in the European Court. It is also possible to challenge the validity of the regulation in the course of national proceedings by making a reference to the European Court (article 177(1)(b)).

References

(1) Case 8–11/66 [1987] CMLR 77
(2) *Confederation Nationale de Producteurs de Fruits et Legumes et al* v *Council*, Case 16, 17/62 [1962] ECR 471
(3) *Plaumann* v *Commission*, Case 25/62 [1963] ECR 95 and 107
(4) Case 64/69 [1970] ECR 221
(5) Cases 41–44/70 [1971] ECR 411
(6) Case 100/74 [1975] ECR 1393
(7) Case 88/76 [1977] ECR 709
(8) [1990] 3 CMLR 946
(9) Case 307/81 [1982] ECR 3463
(10) Case 231/82 [1983] ECR 2559
(11) Case 56–66/74 [1976] ECR 711
(12) Case 74/74 [1975] ECR 533
(13) Case 25/62 [1963] ECR 95
(14) Cases 9, 12/60 [1961] ECR 197
(15) Case 4/69 [1971] ECR 325
(16) Case 5/71 [1971] II ECR 975
(17) Cases 83, 94/76, 4, 15, 40/77 [1978] ECR 1209

QUESTION 5(a)

General Comment

Before undertaking a question such as this you must be sure that you are familiar with the facts and the judgment of the particular case in some detail, as well as knowing the case's importance in the European Court's jurisprudence. All four cases are discussed below, although the question asks the student to discuss only two cases. Please note that 5(d) asks for a consideration of *Defrenne (No 1)* and not the more familiar *Defrenne (No 2)*.

Skeleton Solution

1 The facts of the case

2 Its importance with respect to direct applicability of Treaty articles

3 Its importance with respect to direct effect of directives

4 Its importance with respect to article 48.

Suggested Solution

1 Miss Van Duyn was a Dutch national who had been offered employment as a secretary with the Church of Scientology at its college in East Grinstead. Since the United Kingdom government regarded scientology as objectionable, socially harmful and damaging to the health of its practitioners, it had announced its intention in 1968 of taking all steps within its power – short of legal prohibition – to curb its growth. Accordingly Miss Van Duyn was refused leave to enter the United Kingdom. Alleging violation of her rights as a Community national under article 4 of the Treaty and article 3 of Directive 64/221, she sought a declaration in the High Court to the effect that she was entitled to enter the United Kingdom to take up her employment. A reference was made to the European Court.

2 Under article 48(3), the Treaty provision containing the derogations to the principle of free movement of workers, national authorities must decide what the requirements of the

derogations are. This provision therefore makes the right to immigrate subject to a condition dependent on the judgment of the member state. The question arose whether article 48(3) was directly effective.

As a result of *Van Gend en Loos*, and more recent modifications, academic commentators have concluded that for a provision to have direct effect the wording must be clear and unambiguous, unconditional, and its operation must not be dependent on further action being taken by Community or national authorities (1). Article 48(3) appears to fall foul of these last two conditions. The European Court rejected this and held that article 48(3) had direct effect.

This case can be contracted with *Von Colson*, where a woman who had been refused a job because of her sex, argued that Community law gave her a directly effective right to demand that the Court order the employer to appoint her to the post. The European Court, however, held that there were several ways in which member states could fulfil the obligation to provide a legal remedy. This discretion consequently prevented the obligation from being directly effective.

The difference between the situation in *Von Colson* and that in *Van Duyn* seems to be that in the former the member states had a discretion as to how they would give effect to the right, while in the latter the right was provided by Community law and the member states were merely given a limited power to restrict it in certain circumstances. In the former case the right was incomplete until the member state had acted; in the latter case it was not.

3 The most significant consequence of this case, however, was the attribution of direct effect to directives. In *Van Duyn* the Court was asked whether article 3(1) of Directive 64/221 was directly effective. The UK government argued that directives could not have direct effect since this was apparently incompatible with the wording in article 189. The European Court rejected this submission.

The Court gave three arguments in support of this conclusion. The first was that it would be incompatible with the binding effect attributed to article 189 to exclude in principle the possibility of direct effect. This was a weak argument – it is possible for a measure to be fully binding at an interstate level without its being enforceable in national courts by private individuals.

The second argument was stronger but was based on policy

not law. It was argued that the effectiveness of the measure would be greater if individuals were entitled to invoke it before the national courts.

The third and weaker argument was based on article 177 which grants the Court jurisdiction to give preliminary rulings on, among other matters, the validity and interpretation of 'acts of the institutions of the Community'. The Court argued that this implied that all such acts could be directly effective. In the *Mazlai* case, however, the European Court accepted that it was permissible for a national court to require a preliminary ruling on the validity and interpretation of a Community provision which was not directly effective.

The underlying rationale behind the case is that no government should be allowed to rely on its own failure to implement a directive as a defence against its own citizens. Although this argument was not stated expressly in *Van Duyn*, it has been acknowledged by the Court in later cases – see *Marshall* and *Kolpinghuis*.

The doctrine of direct effect of directives has been refined in subsequent cases. *Ratti* (2) made clear that directives may only be considered for direct effect if the time limit for their implementation has expired. *Becker* said that directives could only have direct effect if their wording was sufficiently clear and unambiguous. *Marshall* confirmed that directives only had vertical direct effect – ie that they could only be relied on by private individuals against the state.

4 *Van Duyn* also threw light on the extent of the discretion left to national authorities under the derogation to article 48. The Court took the view that although article 48(3), as an exception to the fundamental freedom under the Treaty must be interpreted strictly, a member state can, where it deems necessary, refuse a national of another member state the benefit of the principle of freedom of movement for workers even though the member state does not place a similar restriction on its own nationals.

The Court's decision in *Van Duyn* therefore introduced a subjective element into the application of article 48(3) which was apparently at odds with the statement made earlier in the same case that 'its scope cannot be determined unilaterally by each member state'.

In *Rutili* (3) the Court then had to look at the factors which could justify such an exclusion. The Court ruled that a person can only be excluded from another member state if his conduct or presence constitutes a genuine and sufficiently serious threat to public policy. This was subject to the principle of 'proportionality', whereby legislative or administrative action extends only to those measures which are, objectively speaking, least burdensome to those subject to the law.

R v *Bouchereau* (4) added a gloss to the statement in *Rutili*. The requirements of public policy invoked must affect 'one of the fundamental interests of society'. In retrospect, it seems that the Van Duyn decision formulated somewhat generous criteria for the existence of national discretion under article 48(3).

References

(1) Dashwood, 'The Principle of Direct Effect in European Community law' (1978) 16 Journal of Common Market Studies, 229 at 281.
(2) Case 148/78 [1979] ECR 1629
(3) Case 36/75 [1975] ECR 1219
(4) Case 30/77 [1977] ECR 1999

QUESTION 5(b)

Suggested Solution

Despite the central place of the basic principle of the free movement of goods in the structure of the Treaty, it was not until its judgment in the case of *Dassonville* that the Court gave any detailed consideration to the scope of article 30 of the Treaty, and more particularly, gave a judicial definition of the scope of measures having an effect equivalent to quantitative restrictions.

The *Dassonville* case arose out of a prosecution of a father and son who were offering for sale certain bottles of Scotch whisky which they had imported into Belgium from France. It was found that they did not possess the appropriate British customs documentation which would have provided the certification of origin required by the Belgian authorities. The authenticity of the whisky was not disputed but the Dassonvilles had simply placed a label on the bottle bearing the words 'British Customs Certificate of Origin' and a hand written note of the date and number of the French excise bond which had been duly paid. This bond was sufficient documentation for French purposes and the consignment of whisky had been cleared for customs purposes as Community goods on importation into Belgium. Although a direct importer of whisky from the UK to Belgium was able to obtain the requested certification with ease, an indirect importer faced extreme difficulties. The Dassonvilles also faced civil proceedings from the two firms who held the exclusive concessions for Belgium for the brands of whisky involved.

The Court of Justice held that a requirement such as that laid down by the Belgian legislation in issue constituted a measure having equivalent effect, in as much as it favoured direct imports from a member state where the goods were in free circulation.

In a wide statement of principles the Court noted that:

> 'All trading rules enacted by member states which are capable of hindering, directly or indirectly, actually or potentially, intra-Community trade' are to be considered as measures having an effect equivalent to a quantitative restriction.'

This statement requires certain analysis. First of all, it will be clear that although all types of trading rules enacted by member states are covered by the concept of 'measures having equivalent effect', that concept itself has not exhaustively been defined and it is difficult to deduce simply from the phrasing of the basic principle that only rules enacted by member states are covered by article 30. In *Officier van Justitie* v *van de Haar*, however, the Court stated obiter that article 30, unlike article 85, applied only to nationally enacted measures.

Secondly, the Court drew no distinction between equally applicable measures and those applicable solely to imported products. This went further than the position adopted by the Commission in Directive 70/50. Later cases, including *Cassis de Dijon* (1), *Rau* (2) and *Fietje* (3) make it abundantly clear that this approach is correct.

Thirdly, the Court declined to confine the criteria of article 30 to discriminatory measures and instead looked to the effect on trade between member states. This approach foreshadowed the interpretation adopted by the European Court in the landmark decision of *Cassis* which moved the emphasis away from discrimination and towards the protective effect of national rules which excluded from the market of one member state goods lawfully produced and marketed in the territory of another.

Commentators, however, have argued that the *Cassis* judgment seems to be an attempt on the part of the Court to limit the effectiveness of the *Dassonville* rule. It is clear that the exceptions laid down in *Cassis*, the mandatory requirements, can only apply to measures which are indistinctly applicable and the effect seems to be that such measures which are justified by the exceptions are thus taken outside of the scope of article 30 altogether.

Finally, it should also be noted that the existence of one of these mandatory requirements, consumer protection, was also raised in Dassonville. The Court, in dealing with national measures to prevent unfair practices relating to the authenticity of designations of origin of goods in the absence of measures at the Community level, acknowledged the importance of legitimate interests (such as consumer protection) not specifically provided for in Community law. The Court, however, adopted its now familiar approach of insisting that any legitimate interest was subject to a requirement of reasonableness and to a condition that the means of proof required should not act as a hindrance to trade between member states. (See further, *Rau*.)

References

(1) Case 120/78 Rewe [1977] ECR 649
(2) Case 261/81 Rau [1982] ECR 3961
(3) Case 27/80 Fietje [1980] ECR 3839

QUESTION 5(c)

Suggested Solution

Article 85(1) refers to 'agreements etc' which have as their object or effect the prevention, restriction or distortion of competition within the common market'. In *Consten and Grundig* v *Commission* certain of the terms of an agreement creating an exclusive distributorship were held to have the object of restricting competition.

Consten had been given the sole right to sell Grundig products in France and an attempt had been made to provide Consten with absolute territorial protection, which was to be achieved in two ways. Firstly, Grundig undertook not to deliver the contract products, even indirectly, to other traders for export to France. Secondly, Consten was authorised to register in France the trademark GINT which was affixed to all Grundig products. This would enable it to oppose the sale of any parallel imports reaching the French market, as an infringement of its trademark right.

The importance of the *Consten and Grundig* case lies in the fact that it helped to establish an operational framework for article 85(1) by defining some of the terms and requirements necessary to satisfy this article. First, it emphasised that where the implications an agreement may have for competition are not clear, it will be necessary to undertake an analysis of economic conditions on the relevant market to assess the actual extent of any adverse impact. Thus, in the *Grundig* case, by examining the network of contracts between Grundig and exclusive distributors in other territories, all prohibiting the exportation of the products to be supplied, the Court discovered this contributed to the isolation of the French market for Grundig products.

Second, the case appeared to confirm that nothing turns on the distinction between 'prevention' 'restriction' and 'distortion' of competition. The *Grundig* judgment describes the agreement in question as being 'such as to distort competition' while a few lines later it refers to the 'above-mentioned restrictions'.

Third, the case firmly established that the prohibition in article 85(1) applied equally to vertical as well as to horizontal agreements. This was approved by the Court in *Italy* v *Council and*

Commission. A related point, which *Grundig* also makes clear, is that the competition referred to includes competition between products of different brands, as well as competition between distributors of products of the same brand.

The *Consten and Grundig* decision also reflects the curious compromise which has led to the EEC's policy on exclusive distribution. While the benefits arising from such agreements are recognised – the promotion of efficient distribution and the encouragement of new manufacturing entry – and such agreements are not unlawful *per se*, any contract terms or other measures employed to protect the dealer's exclusivity will be condemned as having the object or effect of endangering market integration.

It is not finally settled whether any agreement capable of affecting trade between member states contravenes article 85(1) whenever it restrains competition, even if only in a harmless manner. The Court's case law suggests, however, that article 85(1) must be read subject to a 'rule of reason': an agreement which does not have as its object the prevention, restriction or distortion of competition is unlawful only if its effects are sufficiently deleterious, having regard to the market share of the parties, the existence or absence of a network of similar agreements and the acceptance or prohibition of parallel trading – *Société Technique Minière* (Case 56/65) confirmed in *Brasserie de Haecht*. The Court restated the rule of reason when it held that a selective distribution system was not prohibited by article 85(1) where resellers were chosen on the basis of objective criteria of a qualitative nature and the conditions for the application of such criteria were laid down uniformly for all potential resellers.

More recently, the Court again applied the rule of reason in the case of the dissemination of new technology and the promotion of competition in the Community between a new product and an existing product – *Nungesser and Eisele* v *Commission* and in distribution franchise agreements provided that any restrictions imposed are 'appropriate measures to preserve the identity and reputation of the network which is symbolised by the trademark *Pronuptia* (Case 161/84).

The employment of the concept of the 'rule of reason' means that any agreement is not automatically void under article 85(2). It is also possible to seek to bring an agreement within the block exemption on exclusive distribution agreements in Regulation 1983/84. As Consten and Grundig found to their cost, however, the Regulation reflects the view of the case law that absolute territorial protection cannot be regarded as essential to enable the distributor

to work the market intensively, because some competition from parallel imports was needed to spur dealers on to greater efforts and to prevent them from charging unduly high prices.

QUESTION 5(d)

Suggested Solution

Defrenne (No 1) was one of the earliest cases brought under the equal pay provision of the Treaty, article 119. This case was also the first of three cases brought by Gabrielle Defrenne, an air hostess, against her employer Sabena Airlines. These three cases helped to revolutionise the law in this area.

Ms Defrenne, like all Sabena's air hostesses, was forced to retire at the age of 40. She was then faced with the fact that a Belgian Royal Decree established a pension scheme for 'all members of air crews with the exception of air hostesses'. This special scheme was much more lucrative than the general state pension and was available to the ex-employee when he reached 55; under the general scheme, women could not claim their pension until the age of 60.

Ms Defrenne objected on two counts: firstly her years of service with the airline before the age of 40 were only taken into consideration under the less favourable general scheme; and secondly, she could not claim any pension at all until she was 60. She brought an action in the Belgian courts, which resulted in a reference to the European Court. The national court asked, *inter alia*, whether a pension granted under a social security scheme, financed by workers' and employers' contributions as well as by state grants, fell within article 119.

The European Court held that a retirement pension 'instituted within the framework of a statutory social security scheme' does not fall within the article, partly because the employer's contribution in such a case is not paid directly or indirectly to the worker and partly because the payment does not arise out of the worker's employment. He is entitled to benefit provided that he complies with the statutory conditions. This appeared to mean that discriminatory provisions were permissible in state schemes until outlawed by the third social security directive (not yet in force).

The importance of this case, however, lies in the remarks made by Dutheillet de Lamothe AG. He considered that certain pension schemes are covered by article 119, in particular those which he described as 'supplementary schemes', providing workers in some occupations and in some undertakings with a pension which is added to that paid by the general social security system because in that case the necessary link between the emolument, the employer, the wage or salary earner and the employment appears to be sufficiently established.

The significance of these remarks assumed even greater importance when the ECJ subsequently ruled in *Defrenne (No 2)* (1) that article 119 was partially directly applicable, in the case of direct, overt discrimination (since *Jenkins* (2) and *Bilka-Kaufhaus* (3) the article is also directly applicable in the case of indirect discrimination) and so could be directly relied on by the employee against a public or private employer. Article 119 was therefore used as a means of circumventing the very wide exceptions relating to death and retirement found in the national equality legislation.

Counsel for the plaintiffs in *Worringham* (4) relied heavily on the Advocate-General's opinion in *Defrenne (No 1)*. The employers argued, in their defence, that since the disputed pension scheme was 'contracted out' from the state scheme it related more closely to social security than pay. The European Court, however, ducked the issue entirely and decided the matter in favour of the plaintiffs solely on the narrow facts of the case.

In *Burton* (5), however, a case concerning redundancy benefits which discriminated between male and female employees, the Court tied the voluntary redundancy benefits to the state scheme, a link that the Court did not attempt to draw in Worringham, even though only part of the voluntary redundancy payment contained a pension element. The Court therefore ruled that article 119 did not apply.

In *Newstead* (6), the Court finally categorised the UK system of 'contracted out' occupational pension schemes and substitutes for state schemes and therefore in the nature of social security rather than as related to employment pay. This decision effectively put 10 million employees beyond the reach of article 119.

The most recent decision of the Court on this matter, *Barber* (7), has finally put the record straight by ruling that a pension paid under a private contracted out occupational pension scheme fell within the scope of article 119, meaning that pension benefits must be paid on the same basis to women and men of the same age. The link between social security and occupational pensions had finally been eschewed.

References

(1) Case 43/75 [1976] ECR 455
(2) Case 96/80 [1981] ECR 911
(3) [1986] IRLR 317
(4) [1982] IRLR 74
(5) [1982] IRLR 116
(6) [1988] IRLR 66
(7) [1990] IRLR 240

QUESTION 6

General Comment

A good question for scoring marks – it's worth doing. The following framework will assist you in answering this question.

Skeleton Solution

1 Introduction – area of law, advice to ABC Ltd.

2 Is the measure a) distinctly or b) indistinctly applicable?

3 Does the *Dassonville* test cover this case?

4 a) if the measure is distinctly applicable:
   - i) is the situation covered by article 2 of Directive 70/50?
   - ii) is it covered and prohibited by the case law?
     - – if yes, there is a breach of article 30;
     - – if no, there is no breach.

   b) if the measure is indistinctly applicable:
   - i) is the situation covered by article 3 of Directive 70/50?
   - ii) is it covered by the case law, particularly noting *Cassis*?
     - – if yes, can it be justified by a mandatory requirement? If yes, there is no breach of article 30;
     - – if no, there is no breach of article 30.

5 Is there a justification under article 36?

6 Advise to ABC Ltd.

Suggested Solution

1 Article 30 prohibits quantitative restrictions on imports and measures having equivalent effect to quantitative restrictions. It is intended to prevent such incidents arising as occurred at Dover.

2 All three requirements are indistinctly applicable measures, since the UK law makes no distinction between domestic and imported products.

3 These requirements also satisfy the *Dassonville* (1) test ie 'trading

rule(s) enacted by member states which (are) capable of hindering directly or indirectly, actually or potentially intra-Community trade'. This test is broadly defined (see question 5(b) above) and is proved in this case by the fact that the shipment of goods is refused entry at Dover, thus clearly hindering intra-Community trade.

4b ii) How does the Court apply the *Dassonville* test to indistinctly applicable measures? Prior to the landmark decision in *Cassis* (2) it was generally assumed that article 30 had no application to a national measure unless it could be proved that the measure in question discriminated in some way between either imports and domestic products, or between channels of intra-Community trade. It would be hard to prove discrimination when a national measure applies equally to a domestic and an imported product.

In *Cassis*, however, the Court made no reference at all to the issue of discrimination either because the restrictive effect of national rules made the existence of a discriminatory element irrelevant or presumed it to exist from the very fact of exclusion of products lawfully produced and marketed in one of the member states. This became the dominant attitude of the European Court and was approved by a Commission communication in 1980. *Gilli and Andures* (3) approved this approach and further emphasis was placed upon the protective effect of national rules. In *Prantl* (4), however, the Court combined the notion of protective effect with that of discrimination.

National rules imposing a labelling requirement have been held to fall foul of the Cassis formulation. In *Fietje* (5) the Court ruled that a requirement insisting that the French word 'liqueur' be translated into the national 'likeur' was unnecessary. See also *De Kikrorsch* (6). Article 3 of Directive 70/50 also identifies labelling requirements as potential breaches of article 30.

Packaging requirements are also listed in article 3 of the Directive as potential breaches of article 30. In *Rau* the Belgian government, like the UK government in the case before us, insisted that the product, in that case margarine, be packed in cube-shaped containers. This requirement was considered to be in breach of article 30.

The British government is likely to rely on the mandatory requirement of protection of the consumer as a justification. Article 3 of the Directive, however, insists that the restrictive effect of any measures must not exceed the effects intrinsic to the trade rules – ie the measures must be proportional to their objects and the government must show that the same objective cannot be achieved by other means which are of less hindrance to trade. The case law supports this approach (*Italian Wine* case, *Cassis* for example). As far as the labelling is concerned, the extent to which the label is in French will determine the reasonableness of the British requirement. In *Fietje* the ECJ held that it was reasonable to require some information in the national language on the label. ABC Ltd could argue that an additional label in English should satisfy this requirement. This was the compromise reached in *Prantl*, the *German Beer Purity* case, *Oosthoek* (7) and most importantly *Rau*. The packaging requirement is clearly in breach of article 30 and the justification of the defence of the consumer would not stand up.

The third reason for rejecting the cheese on the grounds that it contains additives which are not allowed in cheese marketed in the UK, is listed in article 3 as a potential breach of article 30. The British government, however, is likely to argue the mandatory requirement of protection of public health, as the governments did in *Heijn* (8), the *German Beer* case, the *Turkies* case, de *Peijper* (9) and the *UHT* case. In the absence of harmonisation rules at the Community level, different standards may apply in different member states as a result of different national value judgments and different factual circumstances (*Heijn* on pesticides) and so the British government can decide that certain additives are dangerous to British health. If, however, it is found that these additives have never been used in British cheese and the measure is simply a disguised way of avoiding article 30, as was the British government's insistence on a slaughter policy to avoid Newcastle's disease in turkies which led to the Turkies case, ABC Ltd can sue the British government for damages for the tort of misfeasance. (*Bourgoin* v *Ministry of Agriculture* (10).)

5 If the British government is unable to prove that its law satisfies one of the mandatory requirements, it is most unlikely to be able to bring itself within one of the derogations listed in article 36.

6 ABC Ltd should therefore apply to the Court for a mandatory injunction or a declaration, seeking a reference to the European Court on matters of article 30 if necessary.

References

(1) Case 8/74 [1974] ECR 837, 852 para 5
(2) Case 120/78 Rewe [1979] ECR 649
(3) Case 788/79 [1980] ECR 2071
(4) Case 16/83 [1984] ECR 1299
(5) Case 27/80 [1980] ECR 3839
(6) Case 94/82 [1983] ECR 947
(7) Case 286/81 [1982] ECR 4575
(8) Case 94/83 [1984] ECR 3795
(9) Case 104/75 [1976] ECR 613
(10) [1985] 3 All ER 585

QUESTION 7(a)

General Comment

This is a lengthy question on articles 85 and 86 and requires careful attention to detail. Provided you have a clear framework in your mind and can remember the salient facts of the key cases you should be all right.

Skeleton Solution

1 Does European law apply – is BB an 'undertaking'?; are alcoholic drinks covered by the EEC Treaty? Do the acts at issue fall within the territorial and temporal scope of the Treaty?

2 Does British Breweries (BB) have a dominant position?

   a) define the relevant market using the material, geographic and temporal criterion;

   b) decide whether BB is in a dominant position by looking at its market share, the share of other participants, the conditions of market entry, financial resources.

3 Is BB abusing its dominant position, if a dominant position has been established?

By answering these three questions you are in a position to answer question 7(a).

Suggested Solution

1 The relevant EEC law is the rules relating to competition in articles 85 and 86 of the EEC Treaty. These rules apply to 'undertakings', a term which is not defined in the Treaty but appears to extend to any entity carrying on 'economic activities' (*AG Roemer Italy* v *Council and Commission* (1)). BB, as a private company, clearly falls within this definition.

These rules cover all sectors of the economy, and the sale of drink is not covered by any of the derogations of the Treaty. We assume these events occur after the Treaty has come into force.

These rules only apply to arrangements which 'may affect trade between member states'. BB could argue that since its activities only take place in the United Kingdom, trade between member states is not affected and therefore national competition law and not European law applies. However, in *Hugin* (2), the leading case in this area, the ECJ stated the test for effect on trade is whether the agreement or practice constituted a threat to freedom of trade between member states in a way that might harm the attainment of the single market, in other words, 'it must be possible to foresee with a sufficient degree of probability on the basis of a set of objective factors of law or of fact that the agreement in question may have an influence, direct or indirect, actual or potential, on the pattern of trade between member states'. (*Société Technique Minière*)(3). The broad wording of this test means that it is not difficult for the Commission to establish an effect on trade – see the liberal interpretation by the ECJ in *AEG* v *Commission* (4). Activities by an undertaking which results in the compartmentalisation of the national market have been found to have an indirect effect on trade eg by making it harder for imports to penetrate the market – see *Cementhandeleren* v *Commission* (5). Specifically, under article 86 the European Court held in *Commercial Solvents Corporation* v *Commission* (6), a case where the dominant company refused to supply chemicals to a smaller company which sold almost all of its production outside the common market, that the requirement of an effect on trade would be satisfied by the impairment of the competitive structure in the Community. A similar test was applied in *Wood Pulp* (7). Thus it would seem likely that European law would apply to BB's actions, unless it could prove that its activities amounted to *de minimis* as in *Hugin* (8). In view of BB's percentage share of the market, this argument is likely to fail.

2 The next task is to establish whether BB holds a dominant position, a term which is not defined in the Treaty but has been interpreted by the Commission in *Continental Can* (9) to mean overall independence of behaviour on the market 'which puts [undertakings] in the position to act without taking into account their competitors, purchasers or suppliers'. Absolute domination is not necessary.

There are two stages to establish a dominant position – a) the definition of the relevant market and b) the assessment of the strength of the undertaking in question on that market.

a) *The relevant market*

It is in BB's best interest to define the product market as broadly as possible – ie as the market for all drinks, alcoholic or non-alcoholic, or at least the market for all non-alcoholic drinks. The court in *United Brands*, a case which turned on whether the banana should be regarded as forming an independent market or formed part of the general market of fresh fruit, adopted the test of limited interchangeability and decided that the banana could be 'singled out by such special features distinguishing it from other fruits that it is only to a limited extent interchangeable with them and it is only exposed to their competition in a way that is hardly perceptible.' (10). The same arguments could be used to distinguish alcoholic beer from non-alcoholic beer, the latter being developed expressly for its non-alcoholic content. Following the Court's reasoning in the *Michelin* (11) case which distinguished the market in retreads from the market in new 'replacement' tyres, it could be argued that although other soft drinks are to some extent interchangeable with non-alcoholic beer, and hence in competition with such beer, sales of soft drinks do not sufficiently undermine the sales of non-alcholic beer, which has been specifically developed for its similarity to beer and not just as another make of soft drink.

From this it can be said that the relevant market is the sales of non-alcoholic beer in the UK at that period.

b) *The criteria of dominance*

The most important factor is the size of the undertaking's share of the relevant market. Market shares have normally been high – in *Continental Can Company* SLW accounted for 70–80 per cent of the market in Germany for meat tins, 80–90 per cent of fish tins and 50–55 per cent in metal closures for glass jars. In *Hoffman La Roche* (12) La Roche held an 80 per cent share of the vitamin market. However, in *United Brands* the Court was content to accept a figure of 'more than 40 per cent and nearly 45 per cent' as constituting a dominant position. The Commission has said that a dominant position will usually be found once a market share of the order of 40–45 per cent is reached and cannot be ruled out in respect of shares of between 20 and 40 per cent.

Furthermore, the rest of the market is likely to be fragmented – CB holds a 25 per cent share and the remaining 35 per cent is likely to belong to smaller producers, thus underlining BB's dominance.

Nothing is known about BB's financial resources or its performance but the above is enough for the Commission to establish a strong case that BB is in a dominant position in the non-alcoholic beer market as required for article 86.

3 To be in breach of article 86 BB must abuse its dominant position. One such abuse is a merger. The EEC Treaty does not contain any explicit merger control provision equivalent to article 66 ECSC. However, *Continental Can Company* established that a merger which causes a dominant position to be strengthened may amount to an abuse. In that case CCC had acquired control of SLW and later TDV. The Commission decided that the merger with TDV amounted to an abuse of the dominant position which CCC held through SLW, because TDV had been a potential competitor of SLW and the effect of bringing it into the CCC group had been to practically eliminate competition. Although the decision was annulled on the ground that the facts had not been adequately analysed the Court confirmed the Commission's view that article 86 might apply in such circumstances.

For a merger to attract the prohibition in article 86 two conditions must be satisfied. Firstly, there must be a pre-existing dominant position to be abused – this has already be shown to be probable in BB's case. It is possible that article 86 also includes the case where a single merger operation between two leading firms results in the creation of a dominant position of such a magnitude as to substantially fetter competition. If BB is not deemed to hold a dominant position its merger with CB would mean that the combined forces of the two undertakings, BCB, would be in a dominant position, although whether a 65 per cent share of the market is of sufficient magnitude is debatable. Article 86 cannot apply to mergers falling short of dominance, even if these seriously affect competition.

Secondly, in *Continental Can*, the Court spoke of strengthening an undertaking's position to a point where all the remaining operators on the market are dependent on it. In the light of developments in cases such as *Michelin* and *Hoffman La Roche* it is unlikely that the Court would insist on a merger having such drastic effect before it would qualify as abusive.

Given this reasoning it seems likely that the BB/CB merger would attract the prohibition in article 86. BB would therefore be well advised to notify the Commission of the proposed merger under Regulation 17 and seek a negative clearance under article 2, to be assured that there are no grounds for intervention.

Two further matters should be noted. Firstly, since the *BAT and Reynold* v *Commission* case, transfers of ownership and in particular minority acquisitions which lead to the coordination of behaviour of independent companies constitutes a breach of article 85. This reasoning could be applied to the British Breweries and County Beers merger. Secondly, as from 21 September 1990, regulation 4064/89 came into force which insists on prior notification to the Commission of mergers, acquisitions and certain joint ventures. The language of the regulation reflects the existing law and the pre-regulation case law will continue to be used extensively. (For further information see Venit, 'The merger control regulation' [1990] CML Rev 7 and Brittan, 'The law and policy of merger control in the EEC' [1990] EL Rev 351.)

References

(1) Case 32/65, [1966] ECR at p418
(2) *Hugin* v *Commission* [1979] ECR 1869
(3) Case 56/65 [1966] ECR 235 at p249
(4) Case 107/82 [1983] ECR 3151
(5) Case 8/72 [1972] ECR 977
(6) Joined Cases 6 and 7/73 [1974] ECR 223
(7) Case 125–129/85
(8) Case 27/28 [1979] ECR 1869
(9) Case 6/72 [1973] ECR 215
(10) Case 27/76 [1978] ECR 157, 272
(11) Case 322/81 [1983] ECR 3461
(12) Case 85/76 [1979] ECR 461

QUESTION 7(b)

Suggested Solution

A further abuse of the dominant position are 'tying' arrangements, as elaborated by article 86(d), where a person is required to accept, as a condition of entering into a contract, 'supplementary obligations which by their nature or according to commercial usage, have no connection with the subject of such contracts'. The requirement that pubs and other purchasers must display prominently BB's non-alcoholic beer and, more importantly, advertising materials appears to satisfy article 86(d). However, such conditions may be examples of tying sanctioned by commercial usage. One commentator has cited the inclusion of a meal in the price of an airline ticket as an example of accepted tying.

In this particular case, however, the advertising goes beyond describing the wonders of the non-alcoholic beer by offering financial incentives towards its purchase, thus locking the consumer into the purchase of one particular brand name, to the exclusion of the smaller producers. The main objection to tying is that it enables a dominant position on market A, the market for non-alcoholic beer, to gain a competitive advantage on market B, the market for alcoholic beer or soft drinks.

If BB is not deemed to be in a dominant position, such contract conditions are likely to fall foul of article 85(1)(e).

BB, however, can try to bring itself within one of the existing heads of the rule of reason and thus argue that the contract does not fall foul of article 85(1). By arguing that these contractual terms were necessary to establish non-alcoholic beer on the market, using analogies with *Maschinenbau Ulm* and *Pronuptia* (1), it might escape the possible contravention of the competition provisions.

Alternatively, BB could seek an exception from liability under article 85(3), by arguing that the contractual terms must contribute to 'improving the production or distribution of goods'. BB is likely to be on weaker ground here, since the Commission insists that the gain to welfare must exceed what could have been achieved without restriction to competition – see *VBBB/VBVB*. In BB's case, competition has clearly been restricted since several small-scale producers have gone out of business – see *Re Ford Werke* (2).

References

(1) Case 161/84 [1986] 1 CMLR 414

(2) [1984]1 CMLR 596

QUESTION 7(c)

Skeleton Solution

1 Does European law apply?

2 Is there cooperative market behaviour?

3 Has competition been prevented, restricted or distorted?

4 If so, does the behaviour fall within one of the block exemptions or rule of reason?

5 If not, what action can BB take?

6 Will GBA's action be caught by an article 85(3) exemption?

7 Are there alternative methods of challenge?

Suggested Solution

1 European law and more specifically article 85 applies to this part of the question. GBA is an 'undertaking' for the purposes of the competition rules and any decision it makes has an impact on BB in Britain, thus affecting trade between member states.

2 GBA is an association of undertakings (breweries) as listed in article 85(1). Its decisions need not be legally binding. In *Re Fire Insurance* (1) the Commission applied article 85 to a 'recommendation', described as 'non-binding' by an association of insurers in Germany, that premiums for various classes of policy be raised by a stipulated percentage. The conclusive factor is the ability of the association, in fact if not in law, to determine its members' and arguably future members' conduct. It is immaterial whether the GBA is publicly or privately established. Furthermore, GBA's rules themselves are a product of an agreement and thus potentially contravene article 85.

3 Article 85(1) refers to agreements etc which 'have as their object or effect the prevention, restriction or distortion of competition within the common market', to an appreciable degree. It is enough that an agreement may have as its object the restriction of competition without this necessarily representing the common intention of the parties (see *Zinc Products* (2) case and *Consten and Grundig* (3)).

Competition is clearly severely restricted if not prevented by the two year trading requirement imposed in Germany. Since most retailers purchase non-alcoholic beer only from the GBA, any new brewery attempting to enter the market would have to trade for two years, selling to a very limited number of retailers – a venture which would not be commercially viable. The two year trading requirement acts as a strong discouragement to new competitors entering the market and effectively closes the market to all but the existing members of the GBA. It is immaterial, since Consten and Grundig, that the arrangement is a vertical agreement between undertakings operating at different levels.

4 Since the two year trading requirement does not appear to be covered by any of the block exemptions or the three 'rule of reason' categories and the sheer magnitude of the domination of the market eliminates a de minimis defence, BB would be advised to make a complaint to the Commission under Regulation 17, article 3(1) and (2). BB is a legal person with a legitimate interest. If the Commission decides not to initiate proceedings and notifies BB accordingly, BB will have sufficient locus standi to bring an action for annulment under article 173. If the Commission takes no action BB can bring article 175 proceedings.

5 GBA would be likely to seek an exemption under article 85(3) on the ground that the two year trading requirement ensures that any new brewer is a reliable, quality producer of non-alcoholic beer, thus contributing to improving the production of the drink, which inevitably benefits the consumer/retailer. These arguments are likely to fail for three reasons. Firstly, the benefit of the two year trading requirement is not strictly economic. Secondly, a two year requirement goes beyond what is absolutely necessary to achieve the objectives regarded as beneficial, and thirdly the measure has resulted in the elimination of some competition.

6 Alternatively, GBA could be regarded as an undertaking abusing its dominant position under article 86 (see part (a) for an elaboration of this approach).

7 Finally, British Breweries could challenge these regulations on the ground that they breach BB's fundamental right to establish itself anywhere in the European Community under article 52 EEC.

References

(1) Case 45/85
(2) Joined cases 29 and 35/83, [1984] ECR 1679
(3) Joined cases 56 and 58/64, [1966] ECR 299

QUESTION 8

General Comment

Unfortunately this question requires a fair amount of technical knowledge about the freedom for lawyers to provide services. Directive 77/249 does help to clarify the situation.

Skeleton Solution

1 Introduction explaining that the legal position is far from clear.

2 The primary legislation – Directive 77/249.

3 The case law.

4 New legislation

Suggested Solution

1 It is not yet possible to make a categoric statement that once a person is qualified to practise law in one Community country, he or she may practise law in any other member state. This lack of clarity is partially due to the uncertain ambit of article 52 right to establishment, which implies a degree of permanence and article 59, right to provide services, which implies a more temporary arrangement. The European Court, however, has stressed the parallels between articles 48, 52 and 59 (*Procureur de Roi* v *Royer* (1)) and that the three articles comprise an integrated whole.

2 Directive 77/249 has helped to clarify the matter. It is concerned with the recognition of the lawyer coming from another member state, as a lawyer, and to afford him the opportunity of acting as a lawyer in the host state. It is thus only concerned with the freedom to provide services (although it has been introduced as a result of articles 57 *and* 66 of the Treaty) and has no effect on the right of establishment in a host state (2), with all the consequent benefits for the immigrant's family. This would require mutual recognition of diplomas etc which have not yet been achieved (cp Directives 75/362 and 75/363 on the mutual recognition of medical diplomas).

The lawyer is permitted to practise in another member state

under the Directive but this freedom is subject to various conditions. Firstly, under article 4(1), activities of representing a client in legal proceedings or before public authorities in a member state must be carried out under the conditions laid down for lawyers established in that state, but there are exceptions against requirements for a residence qualification and the necessity for registering with any organisational body. Article 5 also permits supplementary conditions to be imposed on the foreign lawyer with respect to procedural details consequent to legal representation. Actual appearance before a foreign court is, however, likely to be hampered by linguistic difficulties. Secondly, when giving legal advice, certain basic rules of the host state are imposed on the foreign lawyer in addition to the professional rules of the member state of origin (article 4(4)). Thirdly, the foreign lawyer can be excluded from making wills in the host country and can be refused the right to represent an employer if he is a salaried lawyer-employee (article 6).

3 The utility of this Directive has largely been superseded by the developing European jurisprudence which appears to offer greater freedom to the foreign lawyer. *Reyners* v *Belgian State* (3), the leading case in this area, concerned a plaintiff who was a Dutch national resident in Belgium. He had been born in Belgium, educated there and had taken his Docteur en Droit Belge, only to be finally refused admission to the Belgian bar on the grounds of his Dutch nationality. The European Court held that the prohibition on discrimination contained in article 52, the right to establishment provision, was directly applicable as of the end of the transitional period, despite the opening words of the text of the Article. The court argued that the aim of article 52 was intended to be facilitated by the Council's legislative programme but not made dependent upon it.

The European Court went one stage further in *Thieffery* v *Paris Bar Council* (4). That case showed that even in the absence of directives under article 57, recognition of foreign diplomas may be required under article 52 which prohibits discrimination on grounds of nationality. Thieffery, a Belgian national, held a Belgian law degree recognised by the University of Paris as equivalent to a French law degree. He acquired the qualifying certificate for the profession of advocate, but the Paris Bar Council refused to allow him to undergo practical training on the ground that he did not possess a French law degree.

The European Court held that such a refusal could amount to indirect discrimination prohibited by article 52 of the Treaty.

The next case, *Ordre des Advocats* v *Klopp* (5), appears to put foreign lawyers in a better position than national lawyers. Article 52 et seq were held by the European Court to preclude the denial to a national of another member state the right to enter and to exercise the profession of advocate solely on the ground that he maintains chambers in another member state. (A national lawyer can only maintain one set of chambers within the national territory.) The host state's rules of conduct, however, apply to the foreign lawyer providing they do not discriminate between the national and the foreign lawyer. (*Gulleng* v *Ordre des Advocats* (6).)

Directly applicable rights derived from article 52 secure the foreign lawyer a greater degree of freedom to practise, while dodging the pitfalls arising for rights derived from a directive. Naturally, the derogations to article 52 also apply to the freedom of establishment of lawyers. The 'official authority' exception in article 55 was raised in the *Reyners* case. The European Court, however, while tacitly acknowledging that the occasional exercise of judicial power by an advocate would amount to the exercise of official authority, declared that this would not be the case with respect to the advocate's other responsibilities and so the chapter on establishment applied. Certain functions of notaries public might fall within the ambit of article 55.

4 Directive 89/48 EEC, which establishes a general system for the mutual recognition of higher education diplomas, was adopted by the Council on 21 December 1988. By 1 January 1991 lawyers qualified in the UK and in the rest of the Community will in principle be able to practice anywhere in the Community, provided they have obtained a diploma following a minimum of at least three years university level training, the completion of the relevant professional training and some relevant professional experience in the country of origin or host country.

The Directive permits derogations to the basic principle if there are major differences in the education and training of the migrant and that received by people training in the intended host state. The legal profession is specifically identified as falling into this category so that the 'compensatory mechanism' provisions apply. In the case of lawyers the member state can choose whether the migrant lawyer should satisfy an adaptation period, of a maximum of three years duration or should pass an apptitude test. (See further Wallace, 'Freedom to practice in the EEC', NLJ 21 July 1989.)

References

(1) Case 48/75 [1976] ECR 497
(2) Preamble of Directive 77/249
(3) Case 2/74 [1974] ECR 631
(4) Case 71/76 [1977] ECR 765
(5) Case 107/83 [1985] 1 CMLR 144
(6) Case 292/86 [1988] 2 CMLR 57

UNIVERSITY OF LONDON
LLB EXAMINATION 1991
PARTS I, II
for External Students

EEC LAW

Tuesday, 11 June: 10.00 am to 1.00 pm

Answer *FOUR* of the following EIGHT questions

1 Discuss whether the use which has been made in practice of Article 177 EEC has gone beyond the objectives envisaged for it in the EEC Treaty.

2 Compare and contrast the respective roles of the European Community and the Member States in the areas of (a) the free movement of goods and (b) competition law.

3 Analyse TWO of the following decisions of the European Court of Justice and explain their importance in the development of Community law in the areas to which they relate:

a) Case 27/76 *United Brands* v *Commission*

b) Case 66/85 *Lawrie-Blum* v *Land Baden-Wurttemberg*

c) Case 2/74 *Reyners* v *Belgian State*

d) Case 249/81 *Commission* v *Ireland*

4 What is meant by the expression 'concerted practice', and what role does this concept play in EEC competition law?

5 Pietrasanta SpA is a leading Italian producer of modernistic etchings on a stone background. It contracts with the Rock & Hard Place Cafe in London to supply 10 etchings per month for a trial period of a year for sale in the cafe to customers and passers-by. The first shipment arrives at Southampton in May 1991 but is refused entry by the customs authorities on the grounds that: (a) the customs authorities consider some of the etchings to be pornographic and not entitled under United Kingdom legislation to be sold in the country; (b) the etchings are produced using a chemical which is not permitted for use in any products marketed in Britain; and (c) the products are

produced with a dye which according to United Kingdom legislation cannot be used on products sold in the country because it is deemed to cause serious harm to the environment.

Advise Pietrasanta of any rights which it may have under European Community Law.

6 To what extent is it true to say that the Council is the European Community's legislator?

7 Animus Ltd is the United Kingdom's largest producer of sugar beet pellets, a major component in animal foodstuffs. In late 1990 and early 1991 it invests in new production facilities in order to expand into the French, German and Spanish markets. In April 1991 the EEC Commission makes a regulation implementing an existing Council regulation on animal feedingstuffs. The Commission regulation is based on a background consultancy report originally prepared for the Council, which suggested that Community production of animal feedingstuffs should be reduced in order to allow more imports from abroad and thus encourage the industrialisation of developing countries. The regulation provides for the allocation of quotas to animal feedingstuffs producers by country. The regulation is designed to come into force as of 30 June 1991. Fearing that its substantial investment in new facilities and its anticipated profits may be in danger, Animus consults you regarding its position under European Community Law.

Advise Animus.

8 Discuss the development of the powers of the European Parliament since the establishment of the EEC. To what extent has this development solved the problem of the 'democratic deficit'?

QUESTION 1

General Comment

A difficult question which requires the student to consider not only the relevant rules of law, but also the policy of the European Court towards the development of Community law through the medium of the preliminary reference procedure.

Skeleton Solution

Objectives of Article 177; uniform application of Community law.

The policy of judicial activism on the part of the Court.

Notable cases decided by way of a preliminary reference.

Limitation one: doctrine of acte clair.

Limitation two: the *Foglia* doctrine.

Suggested Solution

Article 177 of the EEC Treaty allows national courts to refer questions of Community law to the European Court of Justice for the interpretation of the Community Treaties and for pronouncements on the validity and interpretation of acts of the Community institutions. Several conventions negotiated among the Member States of the Community, such as the Convention on the Jurisdiction and Enforcement of Judgments 1968, also provide that national courts can refer matters to the Court for a decision.

As the European Court pointed out in the *CILFIT* case (1), the procedure under Article 177 is designed to allow 'the proper application and uniform interpretation of Community law in all the Member States'. This is achieved through co-operation between the national courts and the European Court which ensures that there is little possibility of decisions of national courts on questions of Community law differing from the judgments of the Court on the same point, or for that matter among themselves.

Thus, the preliminary ruling procedure allows the European Court to maintain consistency on both a geographical level and at a jurisprudential level.

Article 177 also imposes on the European Court the duty to supply all courts in the Community with the information necessary to settle genuine disputes brought before them. The Court is ideally suited for this function because it has 'a panoramic view of the Community and its institutions, a detailed knowledge of the Treaties and of much of the subordinate legislation made under them, and an intimate familiarity with the functioning of the Community'; Bingham J, *Customs and Excise Commissioners* v *Samex* (2). These factors give the Court a number of advantages which allow it to effectively discharge this duty.

It is for this reason that Article 177 does not establish a hierarchy between the European Court and national courts. The ECJ is not a final court of appeal for decisions on matters of Community law. Rather, Article 177 is designed to be a mechanism whereby national courts and tribunals can seek guidance from the European Court rather than have a decision imposed upon them.

At the same time, it is clear that the European Court has adopted a deliberate policy of judicial activism. It has rendered many decisions, the reception of which has met with stiff resistance from the courts and institutions of the Member States. The Court has been given the opportunity to consider many fundamental questions of Community law mainly by virtue of the preliminary reference procedure.

For example, two of the most important early decisions of the Court were decided by way of preliminary references. The first, *Van Gend en Loos* v *Netherlands* (3) established the principle of the direct effect of Community Treaty provisions, while the second, *Costa* v *ENEL* (4) allowed the Court to develop the principle of the supremacy of Community law over national law.

The preliminary reference procedure has also allowed the Court to reiterate and expand such doctrines. For example, the Court has developed the notion of the supremacy of Community law to cover even fundamental provisions of the constitutions of Member States as well as long-established constitutional conventions, such as, for example the principle of the supremacy of Parliament; see the *Factortame* case (5).

Without the preliminary reference procedure, the European Court would have been deprived of an important source upon which to draw in the creation of precedents in Community law.

Therefore, clearly the procedure under Article 177 has been more extensively used than was originally envisaged. Further, as the scope of the competence of the Community has expanded into new areas, such as consumer protection, environmental protection, and social policy, naturally more Community legislation has been passed than was originally envisaged. This has, in turn, encouraged the referral of more cases to the European Court.

The volume of references was also not anticipated, as the present backlog of pending cases demonstrates. The average delay between the initial reference of a case and the final decision at present stands at two years, an unacceptably lengthy period for court proceedings.

The European Court itself is aware of the importance of the preliminary reference procedure and has adopted a policy of accepting virtually all cases referred to it by national courts regardless of the merits of the case. Only two limitations or restrictions have been imposed by the Court on the referral of cases under Article 177: the acte clair doctrine and the *Foglia* doctrine.

According to the acte clair doctrine, as developed chiefly in the *CILFIT* case, supra, courts of final instance against whose decision there is no appeal need not refer the case to the European Court if previous decisions of the Court have dealt with the point in contention. However, in discharging this responsibility, the national courts in question are subject to certain duties. First, they must take into consideration the existence of the different language texts, all of which are equally authentic. Second, Community law has its own terminology and legal concepts, many of which differ from those applied in national legal systems. Third, every provision of Community law has to be placed in its proper context and interpreted in light of the system established by the Community Treaties.

The other major self-imposed limitation is that the Court will reject references that arise from circumstances that have been contrived for the purposes of having the Court render a decision that will settle a particular point of law. In *Foglia* v *Novello* (6), a reference was made by an Italian court in a dispute between two Italians concerning a sales contract that required delivery of goods in France. The contract provided that the buyer would not be responsible for the payment of any taxes imposed in contravention of Community law.

The goods were subsequently delivered, but the seller was required to pay a consumption tax in France. He then claimed reimbursement of the tax from the buyer who refused to pay on the ground that the tax was contrary to Community law. The dispute was referred to the European Court.

The Court objected to the reference on the ground that it involved a challenge to the sovereign rights of a Member State, ie the right to tax, in a forum where the state was not in a position to defend itself. In addition, the Court rejected the case because there was no real dispute between the parties. Further, there were grounds for suspecting that the whole transaction had been contrived between the parties for the purpose of presenting a test case to the Court.

A second reference to the Court from the Italian court on the same facts was also rejected on similar grounds. Although the decisions of the Court have been the subject of substantial academic criticism, at the same time it can be argued that fictitious litigation is an abuse of procedure and not the purpose of Article 177. But it must also be conceded that it is difficult to develop reliable criteria for determining the existence of fictitious litigation.

The European Court has certainly taken full advantage of the opportunities presented by Article 177 references to develop Community law. This policy is consistent with the placing of few restrictions on courts and tribunals referring decisions to the Court for consideration. It must therefore be concluded that the use of Article 177 has exceeded the original expectations of the draftsmen who devised it.

References

(1) *CILFIT* v *Ministry of Health* [1982] ECR 3415

(2) [1983] 1 All ER 1042

(3) [1963] ECR 1

(4) 1964] ECR 585

(5) *Factortame Ltd* v *Secretary of State for Transport (No 2)* [1991] 1 All ER 70

(6) [1980] ECR 745

QUESTION 2

General Comment

A comprehensive knowledge of the substantive rules relating to the free movement of goods and competition policy is required before attempting this question. The essence of the question is the division of responsibility between Member States and the Community, a matter that is not extensively discussed in many course syllabuses.

Skeleton Solution

a) Articles 12, 16, 30 and 36 of the EEC Treaty;
the *Cassis de Dijon* ruling;
the test for legitimate mandatory requirements;
the exceptions contained in Article 36;
conditions for the application of Article 36.

b) Effect on trade between Member States;
tests for measuring effect on trade;
co-extensive jurisdiction and examples.

Suggested Solution

a) Member States no longer exercise competence to act in the fields and activities that are stated to be the responsibility of the Community under the EEC Treaty. In the absence of express authority, Member States cannot unilaterally legislate or adjudicate in those fields which fall within the scope of the EEC Treaty.

According to Articles 12 and 16 of the EEC Treaty, Member States are required to refrain from introducing, and must abolish existing, customs duties and charges having an equivalent effect among themselves. These provisions deprive Member States of the right to introduce such duties and also transfer authority to the Community to ensure that these obligations are respected.

Similarly, Articles 30 and 34 prohibit Member States from introducing quantitative restrictions and all measures having an equivalent effect to quantitative restrictions. Compliance with these duties is also compelled at the Community level.

The duty of the European Commission, as representative of the Community, is to enforce these obligations against states. This often involves the initiation of enforcement proceedings against a state in the European Court.

The principal responsibility of Member States is to comply with these obligations to the extent required by the terms of the EEC Treaty. Nevertheless, as these provisions presently stand, the competence of states is not absolutely excluded under the provisions established for the free movement of goods.

Perhaps the greatest role for Member States is the right to enact measures to protect the public against defective or unsafe goods. In the *Cassis de Dijon* case (1), the European Court authoritatively delimited the respective roles of the Member States and the Community in this area.

This case concerned a German law prohibiting the marketing of liqueurs, regardless of origin, with an alcoholic strength of less than 25 per cent. The German government justified the measure as necessary to protect the health of the public and to shield the consumer from unfair commercial practices. The Court accepted the contention that, in the absence of Community measures of harmonisation, Member States continue to retain authority to pass laws and regulations relating to the marketing of products within their territories, but only 'in so far as those provisions may be recognised as being necessary in order to satisfy mandatory requirements relating in particular to the effectiveness of fiscal supervision, the protection of public health, the fairness of commercial transactions and the defence of the consumer.'

A quantitative restriction cannot be justified on any other grounds, unless it benefits from the exceptions to Article 30 specified in Article 36, which also reserves certain rights to Member States as regards the protection of intellectual property rights, the protection of health and life of humans and animals, and the protection of industrial property and national treasures.

Measures introduced as necessary mandatory requirements must serve a purpose that is in the general interest of the Community and be of such a significance as to take precedence over the principle of the free movement of goods, a fundamental rule of the Community.

The first of these tests – in the general interest of the public – was raised in *Torfaen Borough Council* v *B & Q* (2). This case concerned the right of states to impose restrictions on shops to close on Sundays. In principle, such restrictions apply equally between national products and goods of a Community origin.

In considering whether these rules were in the public interest, the Court observed that:

> 'Such rules reflect certain political and economic choices and, in the present state of Community law, regulation is a matter for Member States.'

Therefore, if a matter such as marketing standards remains unregulated by Community law, the Court is prepared to grant Member States considerable discretion in deciding whether such restrictions are to be enacted in the interest of the public.

However, the effects of the national measures should not exceed what is necessary to achieve the goal in mind. National rules that impede the free movement of goods will be declared incompatible with Community law if the measure is excessive in relation to the object of the rule: *Buet and Educational Business Services* v *Ministere Public* (3).

The second test – whether the policy objective of the measure is sufficiently important to prevail over the free movement of goods – is a question to be decided on a case-by-case basis. In the *Torfaen* case, supra, the Court also referred to this test and held that prohibitions of a non-discriminatory character are not compatible with the free movement of goods unless 'any obstacle to Community trade thereby created did not exceed what was necessary in order to ensure the attainment of the objective in view.'

As observed above, Article 36 also reserves the rights of states to introduce legislation designed to protect public health, intellectual property rights, national treasures and industrial property. States may therefore competently enact rules on this basis, subject to several conditions.

In the first place, prohibitions or restrictions authorised under Article 36 cannot constitute a means of arbitrary discrimination or a disguised restriction on trade between Member States. Second, since Article 36 is an exception to the terms of Article 30, it is strictly construed against the party seeking to enforce its terms. Third, the existence of a Community measure on the subject removes the need for additional national legislation. Finally, the reasonableness of a measure is defined in terms of whether it is effective for the purpose claimed and proportionate to the stated objectives.

Subject to these preconditions being met, Member States may continue to enact national rules under Article 36 for these specific purposes.

b) Articles 85 and 86 of the EEC Treaty define the scope of Community competition policy. Article 85 prohibits agreements, decisions and concerted practices that affect trade between Member States and which prevent, distort or restrict competition in the Community. Similarly, Article 86 prohibits any abuse of a dominant position in so far as such abuses affect trade between Member States.

The competence of the Community in competition matters is restricted to anti-competitive behaviour that affects trade between Member States. As the Court itself has pointed out:

> 'It is only to the extent to which agreements may affect trade between Member States that the deterioration in competition falls under the prohibition of Community law; otherwise it escapes the prohibition': *Consten & Grundig* v *EC Commission* (4).

This distinction allows a line to be drawn between unfair commercial practices that have only national ramifications and those practices that have Community implications.

The effect of an agreement on trade between Member States is ascertained by reference to the principle of the free movement of goods and, in particular, the realisation of the creation of a single market among all the Member States. An agreement will affect trade between Member States if it is capable of constituting a threat, either direct or indirect, actual or potential, to the freedom of trade between Member States in a manner likely to harm the attainment of a single market: *Remia BV* v *EC Commission* (5).

The fact that an agreement is entered into by parties in the same state, without involving commercial entities in another Member State, does not exclude the possibility that the agreement might affect trade between Member States. For example, in *Cementhandelaren* v *EC Commission* (6), the Commission found that an agreement between cement manufacturers in the Netherlands was contrary to Community competitive law even although the effect of the agreement was restricted to the Dutch market.

The line distinguishing the jurisdiction of the national authorities and the Community in matters of competition is therefore not clear cut. Because the test for the competence of the Community is based on the effects of agreements, as opposed to, for example, the value involved in a particular transaction, it is not easy to identify practices that infringe Community policy.

At the same time, it is possible that an agreement or concerted practice may fall within the scope of both the national authorities and the Community. For example, in 1988, the Monopolies and Mergers Commission (MMC) conducted an extensive investigation into the practices of the major breweries and in particular into the manner in which public houses are tied to specific breweries. The result was a ruling that certain breweries were required to divest themselves of a certain number of tied public houses.

Following upon the completion of this investigation, the European Commission initiated an investigation into the same subject in the United Kingdom. Despite giving the breweries in the United Kingdom a clean bill of health, the Commission demonstrated that the matter was one which fell within its jurisdiction and was not the exclusive domain of the national authorities.

References

(1) [1979] ECR 649
(2) [1990] 1 CMLR 337
(3) [1989] ECR 1235
(4) [1966] ECR 299
(5) [1985] ECR 2545
(6) [1972] ECR 977

QUESTION 3

General Comment

A question with a considerable latitude given to the student by virtue of the choice of two parts from four. Essentially, there should be no problem tackling these types of problems as long as it is remembered that the examiner is not looking for a narrative of the facts of the case, but rather the relevant legal point and the way that the point has subsequently developed.

Skeleton Solution

a) Relevant market;
dominant position;
subsequent policy of the Court.

b) The principle of non-discrimination;
the problem of vocational training;
expansion of the concept of workers to students.

c) Non-discrimination in the freedom of establishment;
the relevance of harmonising legislation;
discussion of the fact that the case has been largely superseded.

d) Measure of equivalent effect;
requirement of governmental measure;
decision of the Court in R v *Royal Pharmaceutical Society of Great Britain*.

Suggested Solution

a) *United Brands v EC Commission* (1)

The Commission issued a decision stating that United Brands, a company engaged in the distribution of fresh fruit, had infringed Article 86 of the EEC Treaty by abusing its position of dominance within the market by setting prices which bore no relationship to the costs of the product. The case set precedents for two points of law. First, the decision of the Court clarified the test for determining the relevant market for the purpose of applying Article 86. Second, the Court elaborated the concept of dominant position.

Article 86 declares as prohibited, practices that constitute an abuse of a dominant position within a market. Naturally, the definition of market is critical for the determination of abusive practices. For example, if a company manufactures a particular product that itself constitutes a market, it is more likely that its practices will be abusive than if it is only one of many producers manufacturing the product because the share of the product market will be restricted by the existence of other competitors.

In the *United Brands* case, the Court had to decide whether the relevant market was fresh fruit or bananas. United Brands was a market leader in the distribution of bananas. If the relevant product market was fresh fruit, then the position of United Brands in the market for fresh fruit would not be dominant since it was supplying only one type of fresh fruit, bananas, and there were many other types of fresh fruit on the market. On the other hand, if the relevant product market was bananas alone, then United Brands would have a dominant position by virtue of the fact that they were the principal suppliers of that particular product.

In determining the relevant market, the Court held that 'for the banana to be regarded as forming a market which is sufficiently differentiated from other fruit markets it must be possible for it to be singled out by such special features that distinguish it from other fruits.' If a product is interchangeable with others, then the product market consists of the product together with all other products that are interchangeable with it. Interchangeability is defined from the perspective of the consumer according to features such as purpose, taste, price elasticity and appearance.

This test has become the standard for identifying the relevant market. Further, the Court has gradually developed a number of additional criteria for the interchangeability test such as supply elasticity and the importance of brand names: see *Tetra Pak* v *EC Commission* (2), *BBC* v *EC Commission* (3) and *ITV Publications* v *EC Commission* (4).

The second point for which this case is authority is in the identification of dominance. In its decision, the European Court declared:

> 'The dominant position referred to in (Article 86) relates to a position of economic strength enjoyed by an undertaking which enables it to prevent effective competition being maintained in the relevant market by giving it the power to behave to an appreciable extent independently of its competitors, customers and ultimately of its consumers.'

No particular share of the market is therefore required to prove the existence of dominance. In this particular case, the Court considered that a market share of 40% was sufficient but other factors were considered relevant. For example, the fact that the company controlled its own shipping fleet, could regulate the volume of the product entering the Community regardless of weather conditions and had been able to subject distributors to rigorous restrictive covenants, were all considered indicative of dominance.

The Court has continued to develop the factors that evidence dominance in a market. The ability to place obstacles to obstruct competitors from penetrating a market indicates dominance as does the degree of independence enjoyed by the enterprise: see *Eurofix-Bauco* v *Hilti* (5). Similarly, the existence of a monopoly in the supply of the raw materials for the production of a drug was considered substantial evidence of the existence of dominance as regards the distribution of the drug.

b) *Lawrie-Blum v Land Baden-Wurttemberg* (6)

Article 48 of the EEC Treaty establishes the freedom of movement for workers throughout the Community. This has been supplemented by Council Regulation 1612/68 (1968) which gives effect to this right in Community law. Both the Treaty provision and the Regulation prohibit discrimination based on nationality as regards the conditions of employment.

In addition, both provisions rely on the concept of the 'worker' for the operation of the prohibition on discrimination. In other words, a person must qualify as a worker in order to benefit from the protection of the prohibition against discrimination. To determine whether a person is a worker, it is necessary to apply the criteria set by the Community law and it is unnecessary to refer to the terms of the employment contract.

In this particular case, Ms Lawrie-Blum was a British national who was studying in Germany. She was refused admission to the second part of a programme which was a period of probationary service leading to a final examination. The local rules of the district in which she was studying required the possession of German nationality prior to admission to the period of probationary service.

The applicant challenged the refusal to admit her into the next part of the course on the ground that it was contrary to Article 48(2) of the EEC Treaty to discriminate against other Community nationals. The application of this prohibition turned on whether she was a worker in terms of Community law.

The Court held that the concept of 'worker' had to be defined by reference to objective criteria which distinguished the employment relationship by reference to the rights and duties of the person concerned. The essential feature of an employment relationship was that, for a certain period of time, a person performs services for another person in return for remuneration.

Although Ms Blum was essentially a student, she would in fact be subject to the direction and supervision of the school should she be allowed to enter into the period of probationary service. This being the case, the German legislation causing the discrimination was contrary to Community law and therefore inapplicable.

The significance of the case is that it represented a landmark in the Court's policy of gradually extending the concept of workers to persons that would not be considered so within the general meaning of the term. For example, no discrimination can be perpetrated against Community nationals studying in other Member States and such students are even entitled to financial assistance on the same basis as nationals: see *Brown* v *Secretary of State for Scotland* (7).

Gradually the Court has extended the protection of the duty of non-discrimination to an increasingly larger social group, including those not directly engaged in employment. Thus, for example, students can benefit from the rule because they are pursuing a course of 'vocational training' that is an essential part of their training for their careers. In such circumstances, they are entitled to the protection of Article 48(2) even although they are not in immediate employment: see *Blaizot* v *University of Liege* (8).

c) *Reyners v Belgian State* (9)

The plaintiff in this case was a Dutch national who was resident in Belgium. He had obtained a Belgian law degree that entitled him to enter the legal profession in Belgium, but was prevented from doing so by legislation that reserved the legal profession in the country to Belgian nationals. The plaintiff challenged this law as being contrary to the prohibition on national discrimination under Article 7, as applied to the freedom of establishment by Article 52. The matter was referred to the European Court under Article 177.

The Court held that the principle of non-discrimination was fundamental to the functioning of the EEC Treaty and both Article 7 and Article 52 were capable of direct effect. Since these provisions were directly applicable, the Belgian legislation was disapplied to the extent that it infringed these provisions. Consequently, such an impediment to entering the legal profession was held unlawful.

The Court also continued to examine the right of Member States to reserve matters connected with the exercise of official authority under Article 55. In some Community states, such as France, the position of lawyer entails responsibilities as a public official. Belgium contended that, in its territory, lawyers were semi-officials of the state, and therefore it was entitled to rely on Article 55 as an exception to the general prohibition on discrimination.

This argument was rejected by the Court which held that, having regard to the fundamental nature of the freedom of establishment and the rule of equal treatment, the exceptions allowed to such rights in the Treaty could not be interpreted in a manner that would allow Member States to pursue an objective that was disproportionate to the benefits that would accrue.

With the progression towards 1992, the implications of this decision have been eroded. Community legislation has been gradually introduced to harmonise the standards for professional persons such as architects and doctors which facilitate the right of the freedom of establishment. Similarly, rules have been introduced to allow lawyers to practise in different Member States.

Although discrimination on the grounds of nationality is per se prohibited, restrictions on qualifications appear to be acceptable. Thus, a state can reject the qualifications of an individual as being unacceptable to professional bodies. Nevertheless, harmonisation of professional standards reduces this possibility.

d) *EC Commission v Ireland* (10)

Quantitative restrictions and measures having an equivalent effect are prohibited by Article 30 of the EEC Treaty, subject to the exceptions contained in Article 36. The concept of measures having an equivalent effect is not defined in the Treaty, but the European Court filled this vacuum by adopting the following definition:

> 'All trading rules enacted by Member States which are capable of hindering directly or indirectly, actually or potentially, intra-Community trade are to be considered as measures having an effect equivalent to quantitative restrictions': *Dansk Denkavit* v *Ministry of Agriculture* (11).

The concept of measures not only includes all the laws and practices attributable to the public authorities, but also all government funding or approval of activities that have the effect of restricting imports.

In this case, the Irish government funded a 'Buy Irish' campaign which encouraged consumers to purchase goods produced in Ireland in preference over competitive goods from other Community countries. The Irish authorities did not enact legislation or engage in administrative practices to promote the policy, but merely provided finance to private organisations which had been established to promote the campaign.

The Court held that preferential purchasing policies are prima facie measures having an equivalent effect to quantitative restrictions. If a quantitative restriction could be imputed to a policy of the national government and produced discrimination, then it was contrary to the free movement of goods.

This principle has been developed in a number of other cases, the most recent being *R* v *Royal Pharmaceutical Society of Great Britain* (12). In this case, the Royal Society issues directives prohibiting pharmacists from substituting cheaper drugs for brand name drugs, which although prescribed by the doctor, could effectively be replaced by cheaper products. Many of these substitutes came from other Community countries.

This directive was challenged as being a measure having an equivalent effect to a quantitative restriction. The Court upheld the complaint, even though the restriction had not been enacted by the government. If a body is given authority by the central government to regulate a profession, and if this body enacts rules contrary to the principle of the free movement of goods, then these may be struck down as incompatible with Community law.

The important point is that the Court has moved away from traditional conceptions of public acts being considered challengeable under Community law, if discriminatory, towards the notion that the acts of private organisations and bodies can also be so challenged.

References

(1) [1978] ECR 207
(2) [1991] 4 CMLR 334
(3) [1991] 4 CMLR 669
(4) [1991] 4 CMLR 745
(5) [1988] FSR 473
(6) [1986] ECR 2121
(7) [1988] ECR 3205

References (continued)
(8) [1989] 1 CMLR 57
(9) [1974] ECR 631
(10) [1982] ECR 4005
(11) [1990] 1 CMLR 203
(12) [1989] 2 CMLR 751

QUESTION 4

General Comment
A straightforward question requiring elaboration of one of the basic concepts of Community competition law.

Skeleton Solution
Co-ordination of commercial behaviour.

Degree of co-operation required to establish a concerted practice.

The secretive nature of concerted practices and the problem of evidence.

The policy of the Commission and the existence of a presumption given certain circumstances.

Suggested Solution
Article 85(1) identifies three separate practices which may contravene Community competition law: agreements, decisions and concerted practices. Each of these concepts refers to a different form of commercial practice or arrangement among parties.

The term 'concerted practice' refers to forms of commercial co-operation that exist in the absence of a formal agreement. More precisely, a concerted practice, according to the European Court, is:

> '... a form of co-ordination between enterprises that has not yet reached the point where it is a contract in the true sense of the word but which, in practice, consciously substitutes practical co-operation for the risks of competition': *ICI* v *EC Commission* (1).

The essence of a concerted practice is co-operation. Naturally, manufacturers, producers, distributors and suppliers take into account the pricing policies and marketing strategies of competitors when calculating the price of goods and this is an acceptable practice. It is only when a conscious decision is taken to co-ordinate marketing policy that an arrangement becomes a concerted practice.

But, a concerted practice need not involve a detailed and concise plan or strategy. Lesser degrees of co-operation are sufficient. However, some form of direct or indirect contact with the object of influencing actual or potential competition is necessary to establish a concerted practice. Such contacts frequently take the form of negotiations, conferences, discussions, exchanges of views, the swapping of policy documents and communication of market sensitive information.

Concerted practices are only prohibited under Community competition law if they affect trade between Member States and prevent, restrict or distort the conditions of competition within the Community. Only if a concerted practice produces anti-competitive effects can it be challenged under Community law.

A concerted practice will probably be contrary to Community law if it enables the parties involved to secure their positions in a market, or allows them to increase their respective shares of a market. Equally, a concerted practice is prohibited if it interferes with the free movement of goods or diminishes the freedom of the consumer to select between products: see *Sugar Cartel Cases* (2). Also, if parties co-operate to ensure the elimination of all uncertainty in relation to matters such as price increases, supply, and the date and place of changes in marketing strategies, it is likely that the parties will be engaging in unlawful conduct.

The nature of a concerted practice is essentially secretive, and the Commission has largely been engaged in identifying practices, not by way of notification, but after investigations into certain economic sectors. This involves comparisons of actual market conditions with the normal conditions prevailing in particular sectors.

For example, in the *Dyestuffs Case* (3), the European Court held that the Commission had been correct in inferring the existence of a concerted practice from the coincidence of price increases. The timing of such rises could not logically be explained by reference to the normal market conditions of the sector since such conditions rarely, if ever, produced parallel, yet independent, price rises.

Evidence of a concerted practice is usually circumstantial, there generally being no documents to prove the intended course of action. This has led the Commission to assume a policy of requiring undertakings to explain their conduct in suspicious circumstances.

By way of illustration, in the *Woodpulp Cartel Case* (4), the Commission demonstrated the existence of a concerted practice by showing that the price of certain products bore no relationship to either supply or demand. This scenario could not be adequately explained by the parties under investigation. Since commodity prices in general fluctuate wildly in relation to changes in supply and demand, there was a prima facie case of a concerted practice.

References

(1) [1972] ECR 619

(2) [1975] ECR 1663 and [1976] 1 CMLR 295

(3) *ICI* v *EC Commission* [1972] ECR 619

(4) [1988] 4 CMLR 901

QUESTION 5

General Comment

A problem type question requiring the student to analyse the facts presented in the light of Articles 30 and 36 of the EEC Treaty. There appear to be no hidden traps in the question. A familiarity with the basic elements of this part of the syllabus should ensure that a good mark is scored in this question.

Skeleton Solution

Article 36 exceptions to Article 30.

R v *Henn and Darby; Conegate* v *HM Customs.*

Community measures of harmonisation.

German Beer Purity Case.

Title VII of the EEC Treaty and Articles 130s and 130t.

Principle of proportionality.

Suggested Solution

Member States are prohibited under Article 30 of the EEC Treaty from introducing or maintaining quantitative restrictions or measures having an equivalent effect, subject to the exceptions established in Article 36. These exceptions relate to matters such as the protection of intellectual property rights, national heritage and treasures, public health, and also public morality, public policy and public security.

From the facts presented, the first objection of the UK customs authorities is that the etchings in question constitute pornographic material that cannot be sold in the United Kingdom. Article 36 of the Treaty certainly appears to support the right of Member States to reject goods of a pornographic nature and the European Court has allowed a considerable degree of discretion (or the 'margin of discretion') on the part of the Member States to make such judgments.

For example, in *R* v *Henn and Darby* (1), a prohibition on the importation of pornographic materials from other Community countries into the United Kingdom was upheld by the Court despite the fact that such material was freely available in other Member States. The Court is not therefore willing to accept an argument that Community wide standards of morality exist, instead leaving Member States to decide this matter themselves.

There is, however, one exception to this policy on the part of the Court. If a Member State allows the sale of such material within its territory when manufactured by domestic producers, import prohibitions are not justified. This is because permitting import restrictions would allow discrimination in favour of nationals.

Thus, where the importation of erotic inflatable dolls manufactured in the Community was prevented by the British customs authorities, the Court held that the absence of legislation within the United Kingdom prohibiting the manufacturing of such goods created unjustifiable discrimination: *Conegate Ltd* v *HM Customs and Excise* (2). Consequently, a Member State may not rely on the public morality exception to prohibit importation when its own legislation contains no similar prohibition on the manufacturing or marketing of the same goods within its territory.

In the present case, it is likely that the fact that UK law prohibits the sale of these goods would be sufficient to justify the import restriction, although Pietrasanta SpA would be free to argue that the goods in question are not pornographic under the definition provided in the legislation, and on this basis, argue that the import restriction was discriminatory.

The second ground for rejecting the goods is the public health exception also contained in Article 36. Two main principles have been developed by the Court to ascertain whether or not measures to protect the health and safety of the public are justified.

First, the restriction must be necessary for the protection of public health and not a disguised form of discrimination. In the *German Beer Purity Case* (3), the Court held that a German measure prohibiting the import of beers containing additives or preservatives was contrary to Community law because the restriction was excessive and constituted a measure of arbitrary discrimination. In particular, the Court pointed out that, if a product satisfies the health and safety requirements of one Member State, there is a presumption that it will satisfy the standards of other Member States.

Second, the effect of the restrictions imposed must be proportionate to the aim sought to be achieved. The principle of proportionality therefore requires that the power of a Member State to limit imports should be restricted to what is necessary to attain the protection of public health: *Officier van Justitie* v *Sandoz BV* (4).

If the etchings are produced by using a chemical that is banned in the United Kingdom, it is necessary to consider whether the use of the chemical is permitted in other Member States and whether the present state of scientific research into the chemical can justify such a prohibition. Insofar as there are uncertainties at the present stage of scientific research, it is for the Member States to decide what degree of protection is required, having regard to the principle of the free movement of goods.

Thus, if the scientific advisory bodies of the Community have certified that the chemical is safe for this use, it will be difficult for the United Kingdom to justify the ban. Similarly, if there is a Community measure of harmonisation, such as a regulation or directive, authorising the use of the chemical, national measures under Article 36 cannot be justified: *Oberkreisdirecktor Des Kreises Borken* v *Handelsonderneming Moorman BV* (5).

If the etchings are produced in a manner that complies with Community standards, there is an irrefutable presumption that that the goods conform to an adequate standard of quality and safety. In such cases, national measures restricting imports on the grounds of the protection of public health are not justified.

The final ground upon which the rejection of the etchings is based is because the dyes in the product are deemed to cause serious damage to the environment.

National measures to protect the environment are probably justified under Article 36 as necessary to protect public health and, at least until 1986, Member States retained exclusive competence to enact legislation in this field. The Single European Act altered the EEC Treaty by adding Title VII on environmental protection. Article 130s empowers the Council to take action to protect the environment, but Article 130t does not exclude the possibility of more stringent action on the part of Member States.

However, measures adopted by Member States to protect the environment must still comply with the principle of proportionality. Thus, in *EC Commission* v *Denmark* (6), the Court held that a Danish system of requiring manufacturers to package their products in returnable containers was found to be disproportionate to the objective pursued and the restriction of 3000 hl per producer per annum for the production of beer and soft drinks in non-approved containers was contrary to Article 30.

The United Kingdom authorities may therefore justifiably impose such restrictions for the purposes of protecting the environment, but an absolute ban on the use of the dye would have to be justified by a threat of a particularly serious nature.

References

(1) [1979] ECR 3795
(2) [1986] ECR 1007
(3) [1988] ECR 1
(4) [1983] ECR 2445
(5) [1990] 1 CMLR 656
(6) [1989] 1 CMLR 619

QUESTION 6

General Comment

A question requiring a narrative, descriptive answer. In order to score high marks, it is not only necessary to identify the Council role in the legislative process, but also the influence of the other bodies in the procedure.

Skeleton Solution

The strength of the Council's position in the legislative procedure.

The influence of the Commission on the content of measures.

The increasing influence of the European Parliament.

The co-operation procedure and the Tchernobyl decision.

Suggested Solution

There is little doubt that the Council of Ministers is the principal decision-making organ of the Community. As a body composed of national representatives, it embodies the interests of the Member States of the Community and ensures that each state retains a voice in the formulation of Community policy and legislation. Its position in the hierarchy of institutions is such that virtually all the decisions and legislation passed at the Community level must be approved by the Member States through the medium of the Council.

The only limited exception to this general rule is that occasionally the Commission is authorised to enact regulations in particular sectors by the Council delegating authority to act or by the provisions of the Community Treaties. For example, in the administration of competition policy, the Commission retains considerable discretion as to the application of the relevant rules of competition law.

While the Council exercises virtually unrestrained authority to enact legislative measures, this is not to deny that certain constraints are placed on the ability of the Council to influence the content of these rules. The final say in the enactment of Community legislation certainly resides with the Council, but in the formulation of these rules, both the European Parliament and the European Commission exercise some influence.

The European Commission has responsibility for proposing Community legislation and initiating policy. It is the Commission, in conjunction with the various consultative bodies, that constructs draft legislation. Naturally, in the discharge of this duty, the Commission retains considerable discretion as to the contents of a draft measure. At the same time, the Commission is often acutely aware that proposed measures that are too ambitions will be vetoed in the Council of Ministers. In practice, therefore, draft measures are often continuously passed between the Council and the Commission for revisal and modification, a process that dilutes the Commission's influence in the drafting of legislation.

At the same time, the European Parliament has been given a greater role in the legislative process than originally envisaged under the EEC Treaty. Before the Single European Act, the function of the Parliament was essentially advisory. Although some provisions of the Treaty required the consent of the Parliament for the adoption of certain measures, on the whole Parliament could only provide advisory opinions and often the Commission was not even obliged to seek such an opinion, although in practice it often did so.

The Single European Act introduced the so-called co-operation legislative procedure. This procedure extends to the adoption of Community legislation in the following matters: the elimination of discrimination on the grounds of nationality; the free movement of workers and the freedom to provide services; and harmonisation of measures designed to implement the single internal market programme.

Under this procedure, the Commission continues to exercise responsibility for the initiation of proposals which are sent to the Parliament for an opinion before being sent to the Council of Ministers. The Council is then required to reach a 'common position' on the proposed measure, acting by qualified majority. A common position is simply a consensus on the basic elements of the proposal.

This common position is referred to the Parliament which provides the Parliament with an opportunity for a second reading of the proposal. The Parliament has three months to consider its position and to arrive at a decision. If the Parliament approves the measure, or cannot agree on a decision, the Council is free to adopt the measure. If the Parliament challenges the proposal, any proposed amendments are sent back to the Commission which revises the measure in the light of these suggestions. The measure is then resubmitted to the Council which can adopt the proposal (by a qualified majority), adopt the Parliament amendments not approved by the Commission (by unanimity), or amend the Commission proposal itself (by unanimity).

Although the co-operation procedure has increased the influence of the Parliament in the legislative process, it has not eroded the ability of the Council to veto proposals to which opposition exists inside the Council. The general effect of this has been to delay the adoption of certain measures upon which there is no consensus.

The position of the European Parliament in the legislative process has also been strengthened by the decision of the European Court in the *Tchernobyl Case* (1). The Parliament sought to challenge its lack of standing to review acts of the Council under Article 173 of the EEC Treaty. This article reserves the right of judicial review over the acts of the Council to Member States and the Commission.

The Court agreed with the contentions of the Parliament that it should have the right to demand the judicial review of Community acts in which it has an interest. This decision alters the constitutional balance of the Community and represents an endorsement on the part of the Court for a greater role for the Parliament in the legislative processes of the Community.

Reference

(1) (1990) The Times 24 May

QUESTION 7

General Comment

A problem question which presents at lot of information, most of which is relevant to the final form of the answer. In many respects the question itself provides clues as to the answer that the examiner expects. It is therefore necessary to identify the points of law that are raised by the facts as presented in the question.

Skeleton Solution

Article 173(2) EEC Treaty.

Direct and individual concern.

Illegality of the act.

Principle of legitimate expectation.

Suggested Solution

Article 173(2) of the EEC Treaty allows individuals and legal persons to challenge acts of the European Commission. The European Court has exclusive jurisdiction over such actions, and national courts and tribunals may not declare acts of Community institutions invalid without referring the matter to the European Court for a ruling or, alternatively, without there being an earlier decision making such a finding: *Foto-Frost* v *Hauptzollamt Lubeck-Ost* (1).

This jurisdiction extends to acts of the Commission, other than recommendations or opinions. Since, in this particular case, the Commission has adopted the regulation on the basis of the authority conferred by the Council regulation, it is clearly an instrument capable of having legal effects and therefore challengeable.

For the purposes of making such a challenge, Animus will have to establish that the regulation is of 'direct and individual concern', and is contrary to a principle of Community law. Unlike Community institutions, individuals do not have the status of privileged applicants and are obliged to satisfy both these stringent conditions in order to establish standing.

The Commission regulation relating to animal feedingstuffs is not specifically addressed to Animus. Article 173(2) allows a measure of general application such as a regulation to be challenged if it can be shown that the measure, despite its form, is in substance a decision, or a series of decisions, that have been given the form of a regulation for convenience.

For example, in the *International Fruit Company Case* (2), the plaintiffs challenged a regulation establishing a system of import licences to limit the importation of fresh fruit into the Community. Importers could only receive an import licence if the volume of their proposed imports did not exceed a general level. The Court upheld the plaintiff's argument on the grounds of jurisdiction on the basis that the regulation was not a generally applicable measure, but rather a 'conglomeration of individual decisions taken by the Commission under the guise of a regulation'. Animus would have to prove that the regulation is in fact a 'conglomeration of individual decisions'.

If Animus is successful in demonstrating that the regulation is a decision, it must prove that the decision is of both direct and individual concern. Direct concern requires that the Community measure being challenged must affect the applicants without the intervention of the state authorities. If national authorities have a discretion as to the method of implementing a regulation, or are involved in the administration of the terms of the regulation, direct concern cannot be established. Thus, in *Bock* v *EC Commission* (3), the Court refused standing because the implementation of the Community measure allocating quotas actually depended on the distribution of the allowances by the individual states.

But, where the national authorities have no discretion in implementing a Community measure, direct concern may be established; *Sofrimport Sarl* v *EC Commission* (4). In other words, where the hands of the national authorities have been tied by the Council or Commission, then responsibility for the act may be imputed to these institutions. This is a critical issue in the present circumstances, because according to the facts presented in the question, the quotas are allocated by country, suggesting de facto national administration.

The test for individual concern requires the applicant to prove that the measure affects its legal position 'because of a factual situation which differentiates them individually in the same way as to the person to whom it is addressed': *Sociedad Agro-Pecuaria* v *EC Council* (5). In other words, the decision must affect the applicant in some specific manner, and not generally, as for example, in common with all other Community producers.

Individual concern is difficult to establish, but has been demonstrated where regulations name specific undertakings and apply particular measures to them and where the decision was issued by the Commission in response to the requests of an identifiable group one member of which is the applicant.

From the facts presented, the regulation was adopted on the basis of a background report submitted to the Council. The case for standing would be enhanced if Animus was a contributor to the report and its suggestions formed the basis of the proposal. This is unlikely since the report indicates that quotas should be introduced to encourage imports from developing countries at the expense of Community producers.

If Animus was specifically identified in the regulation by name, then there would also be a strong case for individual concern. But, it appears that the regulation applies to objectively determined situations and entails legal effects for general categories of Community producers.

A further hurdle to proving individual concern is that Animus manufactures sugar beet and not the relevant animal foodstuffs. Animus therefore manufactures merely a component of the final product, a factor that will count against it being able to prove direct concern.

If Animus is successful in establishing standing, it would also have to establish that the Commission regulation was unlawful because it is incompatible with Community law. There are a number of grounds upon which such an argument could be made.

First, the regulation is based on an existing Council regulation. Presumably the Commission was authorised to adopt the regulation by the delegation of authority contained in this decision. Animus may be able to argue that the regulation may be annulled on the basis of the lack of competence of the Commission to adopt such a measure. It would be necessary to establish that the Commission had acted ultra vires, and outside its authority.

Second, annulment of a Community act is possible if an institution has infringed an essential procedural requirement, but annulment is only possible if the procedural error is substantial or involves an important stage in the decision-making processes leading to the adoption of the decision: *Dyestuffs Case* (6).

Third, and most extensively, the regulation may be annulled if it infringes the provisions of the Community Treaties or any of the rules relating to its application. This ground is most often used to challenge decisions involving violations of the fundamental principles of Community law, misinterpretations of the Community Treaties and errors in establishing facts.

Prima facie, it appears that an argument may be made that the regulation infringes two principles of Community law: the doctrine of legitimate expectations and the principle of proportionality.

Animus has made a large investment of funds on the assumption that Community law, as it stood prior to April 1991, did not impose restrictions on the development of production. The question is whether Animus had a legitimate expectation that its investment would not be threatened by Community legislation. Most of the cases in which the principle has been applied turn on the fact that the Community has held out certain information or facts upon which an individual has based their decision, and then subsequently undermined the financial position of the individual by compromising their position. Thus, in *Mulder* v *Minister van Landbouw* (7), the Court held that a farmer who had accepted Community payments for suspending production in return for annual repayments, could not be excluded from the subsequent allocation of quotas at the end of the scheme.

The other principle, that of proportionality, requires that the effects of measures introduced by the Community must remain in proportion to the objectives sought. Animus could therefore argue that the foreclosing of the market for feedstuffs in the Community is excessive in relation to the objective pursued, namely the stimulation of imports from developing countries.

References

(1) [1988] 3 CMLR 57
(2) [1971] ECR 41
(3) [1971] ECR 897
(4) [1990] 3 CMLR 80
(5) [1990] 1 CMLR 105
(6) *ICI* v *EC Commission* [1972] ECR 619
(7) [1989] 2 CMLR 1

QUESTION 8

General Comment

An essay-type question dealing with a popular and recurring theme. It should not be difficult to score highly on such a question.

Skeleton Solution

Original powers of the Parliament.

Powers under the Single European Act.

The decisions of the European Court.

The direction of the present inter-governmental discussions on political integration.

Suggested Solution

The role of the European Parliament in the operation of the Community has always been advisory and consultative rather than legislative. In contrast to the role of the democratic legislative organs in the legal systems of the Member States, the function of the Parliament has been restricted since its conception. Despite the powers vested in the Parliament after the amendments made to the EEC Treaty by the Single European Act, it is impossible to claim that the Parliament has as much political or legal control over the legislative process as its counterpart institutions within the Member States.

Although members of the European Parliament have been elected by direct universal suffrage throughout the Community since 1979, effective power and control has never been vested in the Parliament. In fact, the Parliament has had to contend with a variety of diverse powers that have been conferred to impede abuse of power in the Council and the Commission rather than as a result of the desire to confer the institution with authority to represent the population of the Community. It is also clear that the Parliament's authority over the Commission is greater than over the Council, where in fact ultimate legislative capacity continues to reside.

The European Parliament was originally conferred with authority to oversee the activities of the Commission. First, the Commission is required to answer questions posed by Members of the European Parliament. Both written and oral questions may be submitted. Clearly,the Commission takes this power very seriously, and considerable effort is spent in preparing answers to question from both plenary sessions and the committees of the Parliament. In part this is due to the view on the part of the Commission that the Parliament is an ally in the quest for greater delegation of authority to the Community.

The Commission is also obliged to submit an annual general report to the Parliament on the affairs of the Community, which is then discussed in an annual parliamentary debate. In the event that the Parliament is dissatisfied with the performance of the Commission, it may dismiss the Commission by a motion of censure carried by a two-thirds majority. However, since the Commission is a collegiate body, all the Commissioners must be dismissed and the Parliament has no authority to dismiss an individual Commissioner.

The Parliament also exercises a number of general powers. Together with the Commission, it prepares the Community budget for submission to the Council of Ministers, but the Parliament may only approve or modify certain budgetary items depending on the type of expenditure involved. Where the expenditure is obligatory, for example for compensation under the Common Agricultural Policy, Parliament may only alter the item with the consent of the Council. But, where the expenditure involved is non-obligatory, the Parliament has automatic authority to modify items, subject to restrictions on increases.

It is true that the Single European Act did create additional powers for the Parliament. For example, the consent of the Parliament is required under Article 237 of the EEC Treaty for the admission of new members. Similarly, consent is also required for the conclusion of agreements between the Community and other states.

In at least one case the Parliament has refused to consent to the ratification of an agreement. In 1987, Parliament withheld its consent to ratify a bilateral trade agreement between the Community and Israel in protest at the treatment by the Israeli authorities of Arabs in the occupied territories. Indeed, this is an effective power and, for example, the Parliament will have an important say in the conclusion of the multitude of agreements that will form the final settlement of the Uruguay Round of multilateral trade negotiations under the auspices of the GATT. Also, the Parliament is required to give its assent to the ratification of the treaty negotiated in October 1991 between the Community and the EFTA countries creating the European Economic Zone.

The other important concession granted by the Single European Act was the so-called 'co-operation' procedure introduced for the passage of certain types of legislation, including all the regulations and directives required for the completion of the single internal market programme. Prior to 1986, the Commission was only required to seek an opinion from the Parliament in certain areas, but in practice often sought its opinion during the legislative process. Since 1986, the Commission is required to seek the views of Parliament for decisions relating to its former powers as well as under the co-operation procedure.

Yet, the Parliament is conscious of the fetters that have been imposed upon it and has relied extensively upon the sympathies of the European Court to strike a more even balance in the distribution of effective supervisory power. In a number of important cases, the Court has extended the powers of review of the Parliament. For example, in the *Tchernobyl Case* (1), the European Court reversed a long-standing series of precedents and established the principle that the Parliament has standing to challenge acts of the Council that adversely affect its position.

At the same time, the impotence of the Parliament was demonstrated by the series of decisions concerning the location of the Parliament itself. In these cases, the Court denied power to the Parliament to decide its own seat and held a resolution calling for a single location invalid: *Luxembourg* v *European Parliament* (2).

Despite the pretensions of the Members of Parliament themselves, at the moment the Parliament remains little more than a talking shop. It is a forum for discussion, for the airing of views and for the exchange of information. Although on occasion resolutions of the Parliament have provided the impetus for draft legislation from the Commission, most parliamentary resolutions have little effect and are not even commented upon by the press. Indeed, judging from the content of many such resolutions, it is not clear whether the Parliament considers itself bound to confine itself to discussions on subjects that fall within the competence of the European Community.

In the final analysis, the so-called democracy deficit within the Community has not been solved by the amendments made by the Single European Act, and pending the outcome of the discussions on political integration presently being conducted at the intergovernmental level, continues to remain as wide as when the Community itself was conceived. The Community is structured on the principle of vested interests, not democracy. The Council represents the interests of the Member States, and the Commission the interests of the Community. The role of the Parliament is to voice the concerns of the European population, but it has not been given effective powers to do so. The result is a constitutional structure which bears no relationship to the principles of democracy.

Whether the democratic deficit will be narrowed depends largely on the results of the discussions on political co-operation. The British government opposes granting more powers to the Parliament and, in contrast, the German government enthusiastically supports transferring such powers. In the end, the nature of the final compromise reached will indicate whether or not the Community is to be based on the democratic ideals that feature so greatly in many of the constitutions of its Member States.

References

(1) (1990) The Times 24 May
(2) [1983] ECR 255

UNIVERSITY OF LONDON
LLB EXAMINATION 1992
PARTS I, II
for External Students

EC LAW

Tuesday, 9 June: 10.00 am to 1.00 pm

Answer *FOUR* of the following EIGHT questions

1 Analyse Case 26/62 *Van Gend en Loos* and discuss its significance for the effective enforcement of European Community Law.

2 To what extent does Article 189 EEC provide an accurate description of the acts which may be taken by the European Community institutions? What suggestions would you make regarding the possible redrafting of Article 189 EEC?

3 It has been suggested that Article 85 EEC is intended only to support the rules for the movement of goods. Comment on this suggestion in the light of the case law of the European Court of Justice, particularly the judgment in *Consten & Grundig* v *Commission*.

4 What role does the Commission play in the European Community's legal and institutional structure? What are the principal factors which have influenced the development of its role since 1958?

5 Discuss the purposes of Article 177 EEC and evaluate the extent to which these purposes have been achieved. To what extent is Article 5 EEC a necessary complement to Article 177 EEC?

6 Martin NV exports TV aerials from the Netherlands to the United Kingdom. It enters into a contract with Nairn Ltd to supply 1,000 aerials a month. The first shipment from Martin to Nairn is stopped by United Kingdom customs authorities. The authorities state that:

a) United Kingdom law requires that such products be inspected at the port, the inspection has been carried out and a fee is now due;

b) the aerials are made partly of an aluminium alloy which United Kingdom legislation prohibits from being used in the United Kingdom for reasons of consumer protection;

c) the strength of the aerials is below that required by standards adopted by the United Kingdom pursuant to the procedure permitted by Article 100A(4).

Advise Martin NV as to any rights and remedies which it may have under European Community law.

7 To what extent is it true to say that if a person is admitted to the practice of law in one Member State, he or she is entitled to practise in all the other Member States?

8 Discuss the legal principles which form the basis of the European internal market envisaged by Article 8A EEC and evaluate the legislative mechanisms available for the implementation of these principles. In your answer you should also consider what other legal means, if any, might be necessary to achieve European economic integration.

QUESTION 1

General Comment

This question concerns one of the fundamental decisions of the European Court on Community constitutional law and naturally students should be aware of its significance. To score well, it is necessary to comment effectively on the constitutional impact of the decision as well as the subsequent developments which have followed since the judgment of the Court in this case.

Skeleton Solution

The principle of direct effect elaborated by the court in the decision.

Policy reasons behind the elaboration of this principle.

Subsequent development of the principle of direct effect by the court in later cases.

The limits of the court's decision as regards the failure to state a principle of supremacy.

Suggested Solution

The draughtsmen of the EC Treaty envisaged the creation of a supranational institution based on the rule of law. The establishment of a European Court to adjudicate disputes arising among Community institutions, Member States and, in certain cases, private individuals, indicates the importance of this principle. In the performance of this function, the Court is instructed to ensure respect for the rule of law in the interpretation and application of Community law.

While the Court is obliged to ensure the proper enforcement of Community law, there are no provisions specifically referring to the means through which this objective is to be achieved. For example, the EEC Treaty does not refer to the possibility of fines or the suspension of the rights of Member States in the event of an infringement of Community law. Judgments of the European Court, in direct actions at least, are declaratory in nature and although Member States are required under article 5 to ensure the 'fulfilment of the obligations arising out of the Treaty', there is no express provision regarding sanctions.

Naturally, this omission gave rise to concerns that the effective enforcement of Community law would be impaired if the rights and duties established under the Treaty only applied to the relationships between Member States inter se on the one hand and between the individual Member States and Community institutions on the other hand. The extension of these rights and duties to individuals provided a means whereby the effectiveness of Community law could be enhanced simply by allowing private individuals access to processes which would allow them to exercise these rights.

Such an extension would have two immediate effects. Firstly, it would alleviate the need for individuals to petition their Member States for the enforcement of rights at the Community level. Secondly, it would rapidly expand the scope of Community law as far as the number of subjects, ie Member States, Community institutions, private individuals, legal persons etc, to which Community law applied.

In the early years of its jurisprudence, the European Court was clearly concerned that the effective enforcement of Community law was only possible, first, if individuals were allowed to rely on provisions of Community law and, second, if Community law prevailed over inconsistent provisions of national law. It has been this concern that has been the motive for much of the judicial activism of the court.

The creation of private rights has the effect of dispensing with the need for a central body to supervise the enforcement of Community law by bringing Member States before the European Court. True, the European Commission is empowered to bring Member States before the court for breaches of Community law by means of direct actions. But, particularly in light of the dramatic growth in the scope of Community law, it is clearly impossible to require the Commission to act against each and every infringement. Allowing individuals to do so in their own national courts relieves the Commission of a substantial part of this responsibility, which increases the degree of effective enforcement.

The Court has primarily contributed to the effective enforcement of Community law in two ways. It has encouraged national courts to apply Community law and, secondly, it has allowed individuals to rely on Treaty provisions for enforceable private rights. The Court's policy in this respect was clearly manifested in *Van Gend en Loos* (1), a case in which the European Court decided that private individuals could rely on the express terms of the EEC Treaty as a ground for action in their national courts.

The facts of the case may be briefly stated as follows. Under Dutch customs law, a particular chemical was subject to an ad valorem duty of 3 per cent on importation at the time the EEC Treaty entered into force. This duty was permitted on intra-Community trade as an interim measure pending the transition of the Community to an area free of customs duties.

In the following year, the Dutch government reclassified the chemical into another customs heading which attracted a customs duty of 8 per cent instead of 3 per cent. A German manufacturer challenged this increase in duty as being contrary to article 12 of the EEC Treaty which requires Member States to refrain from introducing any new customs duties on imports or exports and from increasing those duties which operated at the time the EEC Treaty came into effect.

The matter was referred to the European Court from the Dutch court for a preliminary ruling. The main question was whether article 12 was capable of being given direct effect thereby allowing private individuals to rely on its terms before national courts and tribunals.

At the outset of the case, the government of the Netherlands disputed the Court's jurisdiction to answer this question on the ground that the matter was one of Dutch constitutional law. The Court rejected this argument quite simply because the case concerned the interpretation of a provision of the EEC Treaty, namely article 12.

The Court then went on to consider the question of the direct effect of article 12. To decide this issue, the Court looked at the purpose as well as the terms of the EEC Treaty itself. It noted that the purpose of the Treaty was not only to establish mechanisms for co-operation between Member States but also to provide individuals with enforceable rights. For example, the purpose of article 177 was to ensure uniformity of interpretation on the Treaty by national courts which strongly suggested that the Member States recognised that Community law could be invoked by nationals before national courts.

From this the Court concluded that 'the Community constitutes a new legal order in international law, for whose benefit the States have limited their sovereign rights, albeit within limited fields, and the subjects of which comprise not only the Member States but also their nationals.' From a constitutional perspective, this statement forms the foundation on which the present framework of European Community law stands.

The significance of this decision stems from its relevance for effective enforcement. In the absence of some form of direct effect, individuals would be unable to raise private actions in national courts to assert their Community rights. National courts, frequently with the assistance of the European Court through the preliminary reference procedure, have contributed immensely to the enforcement of Community law. Instead of only one court capable of ruling on points of Community law, all the courts of the 12 Member States can competently consider questions of Community law by virtue of the principle of direct effect.

In a number of subsequent decisions the Court has gone much further in asserting the principle of direct effect. For example, in addition to the direct effect of Community regulations expressly recognised in article 189 of the EEC Treaty, the Court has also extended the principle of direct effect to unimplemented Community directives and certain international agreements entered into by the Community with third states. While the direct effect of both treaty provisions and the terms of Community directives is subject to a number of conditions, nevertheless, the evolution of the principle has been significant for the effective enforcement of Community law.

In the *Van Gend en Loos* case, the principle of direct effect was not accompanied by its logical corollary, namely the principle of the supremacy of Community law. Failure to declare that directly applicable rules of Community law prevailed over inconsistent rules of national law could have had a potentially limiting effect on the effective enforcement of Community law. But the Court quickly remedied this deficiency in its decision in *Costa* v *ENEL* (2), which followed in the next year.

In this case, the Court asserted that Community law prevailed over national legislation whether enacted before or after membership of the Community. The participation of the Member States in the Community limited the rights of these countries to enact legislation contravening the terms and the spirit of the Treaty.

To ensure the effective and consistent application of Community law in all Member States, it was essential that Community law prevailed over national measures. If the reverse was the case, Community law would be deprived of all its imperative strength and its effective enforcement could not be guaranteed. Hence, the Court held that:

> 'the law stemming from the [EEC] Treaty, an independent source of law, cannot, because of its special and original nature, be overridden by domestic legal provisions, however framed, without being deprived of its character as Community law and without the legal basis of the Community itself being called into question.'

Subsequently, the principle of the supremacy of Community law has been extended to cover not only provisions of the Community Treaties but also Community regulations and, in certain instances, Community directives.

References

(1) [1963] CMLR 105
(2) [1964] CMLR 425

QUESTION 2

General Comment

This question concerns the changes brought about through the intervention of the European Court to the various types of measures that can be enacted by Community institutions. While a descriptive answer is required, the question also calls for the views of the student on the present terms of a particular provision of the EEC Treaty which is, of course, quite challenging in exam room conditions.

Skeleton Solution

The terms of article 189: regulations, directives, decisions and recommendations.

Regulations: direct effect/binding in their entirety.

Directives: no express direct effect but note the rulings of the ECJ.

Blurring of the distinction between regulations and directives.

Redrafting proposals: define the various types of measures in light of the jurisprudence of the ECJ.

Suggested Solution

Article 189 of the EEC Treaty identifies five different types of measures that may be adopted by the Council of Ministers and the European Commission in the performance of their functions and legal duties. Both organs are permitted to make regulations, issue directives, take decisions, make recommendations and to deliver opinions. Of these, only regulations, directives and decisions have legal effects. Neither recommendations nor opinions have binding legal force.

In practice, regulations and directives are the most important types of acts or measures that can be enacted at the Community level. Decisions, while common in some fields such as competition law, are not a major form of Community measure. Decisions are binding in their entirety, but only upon the entity to whom they are addressed. Decisions may be addressed to Member States but most frequently they are applied to individuals and legal persons.

The description of regulations and directives in Article 189, however, no longer adequately describes the two principal measures used by the Community institutions. It is in this respect that it is open to speculation whether or not article 189 continues to accurately define the measures that may be taken by Community institutions.

A Community regulation is a general legislative instrument which is binding in its entirety throughout the Community, unless otherwise stated, and which is directly applicable within the legal systems of the individual Member States without the need of intervention on the part of national legislative bodies. Individuals may therefore rely on the terms of a regulation in a national court even though there is no national law giving it effect. The English courts have acknowledged this quality and have been prepared to recognise the force of Community law in this form and to protect individual rights vested in this manner: *R* v *Secretary of State, ex parte Factortame* (1).

Regulations are therefore clearly designed as measures permitting the Community institutions to legislate directly throughout the whole of the Community. This purpose is recognised in s2(1) of the European Communities Act 1972 which requires that all rights and obligations created in accordance with the Community Treaties are 'without further enactment to be given legal effect' within the United Kingdom.

True, occasionally Community regulations are re-enacted by measures of national law to provide greater clarity or to create penalties for failure to comply with the terms of a regulation. However, in such cases, the force of law continues to reside in the regulation and is not superseded by the national measure. Further, if a regulation is so re-enacted, the legislation must satisfy all the obligations incumbent on the Member State. Partial implementation is insufficient.

Thus, in *EC Commission* v *United Kingdom (Re Tachographs)* (2), the United Kingdom was held in violation of a Community regulation requiring the fitting of tachographs to certain types of vehicle. The regulation required the creation of criminal sanctions for failure to do so but the implementing legislation enacted in the United Kingdom made no such provision. The European Court held the United Kingdom liable for breach of the EEC Treaty and declared that it was inconceivable that a Member State could implement a regulation 'in an incomplete or selective manner ... so as to render abortive certain aspects of Community legislation which it opposed or which it considered contrary to its national interests'.

Regulations are therefore the most effective and comprehensive measures that may be adopted by Community institutions. Directives, on the other hand, are expressly declared in article 189 to have binding effect, but only as against the Member States to whom they are addressed. More importantly, the text of article 189 implies that directives are not directly effective because the national authorities of each Member State exercise a discretion in selecting the appropriate measure of national law to give effect to the terms of the directive. Directives are therefore, at the same time, less comprehensive in their coverage than regulations and also lack the automatic effect possessed by regulations.

However, the distinction between these two types of measures is no longer clear cut and arguably article 189 requires redrafting to reflect this fact. There has developed a blurring in both function and effect of regulations and directives caused, for the most part, by the desire on the part of the European Court to render directives more effective.

The European Court has been prepared to give vertical direct effect to directives that have remained unimplemented by Member States after the period provided for the adoption of the directive. In other words, the Court has been prepared to refuse to allow the failure of a state to adopt a directive as an excuse to an otherwise competent action. As the Court pointed out in *Grad* v *Finanzamt Traunstein* (3):

> 'It would be incompatible with the binding effect given by article 189 [of the EEC Treaty] to directives to refuse in principle to allow persons concerned to invoke the obligation imposed by the directive ... Especially in cases where the Community authorities, by means of a directive, oblige Member States to take a specific course of action, the practical effectiveness of such a measure is weakened if individuals cannot take account of it as part of Community law.'

But the right to rely on the terms of an unimplemented directive is not absolute. Three conditions must be satisfied before reliance can be placed in the measure. First, the terms of the directive must be sufficiently precise to create directly enforceable legal obligations. Second, the provision must specify an obligation which is not subject to any qualification, exception or condition. Third, the provision must not require intervention on the part of a Community institution or a Member State. These are the necessary preconditions for a regulation to be considered as having direct effect.

There are, however, two major limitations placed on the application of this principle.

Firstly, the principle applies only to directives which remain unimplemented after the date has passed for adoption. The entry into force of directives which have been adopted, but which have not yet entered into force, cannot be anticipated or pre-empted.

Secondly, and more importantly, the Court has only been prepared to apply this doctrine to the relationships between individuals and the state as opposed to the relationships among individuals themselves. In other words, while an individual can evoke an unimplemented directive against national authorities, either as a ground for action or a defence, the rights conferred by the directive cannot be enforced against other individuals. Thus, in *Marshall* v *Southampton and South West Hampshire Area Health Authority* (4), the Court refused to allow the principle of direct effect to be used by an employee suing her employer for failure to comply with directives concerning equal pay.

The situation has, however, been made even more complex by recent decisions of the Court which, while continuing the policy of refusing to give horizontal direct effect to directives, have nevertheless opened up the possibility of an alternative remedy in such cases. First in *Von Colson* v *Land Nordrhein-Westfahlen* (5), and more recently in *Marleasing SA* v *La Commercial Internacional De Alimentacion SA* (6), the Court has given indirect horizontal effect to directives by means of article 5 of the EEC Treaty. This article requires Member States to take all appropriate measures to ensure the fulfilment of the obligations arising out of the EEC Treaty.

In the *Marleasing* case, the plaintiffs alleged that a Spanish company had been wound up for the purpose of defrauding its creditors. The company was formed by a founders contract which is an agreement among the participants in the company to establish a company. This was a legitimate means of establishing a company under Spanish law. The plaintiffs claimed that the founders contract was void for lack of consideration, a concept recognised in Spanish company law, and therefore the directors would be liable for its debts.

The grounds on which a company can be annulled are exhaustively listed in Directive 68/151. Lack of consideration is not a ground listed in this directive but the Spanish government had not implemented its terms at the time the dispute arose. The defendants relied on this directive to support the claim that the company could not be wound up for lack of consideration because this was not a ground for declaring a company void under the directive. The Court was asked whether the directive could be given effect as between these two private parties.

While the Court rejected the notion of horizontal directive effect, it observed that article 5 places Member States under an obligation to give effect to Community obligations. Spanish law had to be interpreted in light of this obligation and this required that Spanish company law should be interpreted in light of the terms of the directive. Since the directive exhaustively listed all the grounds for annulling a company, the Spanish company could not be annulled for lack of consideration.

The effect of this decision is to give indirect horizontal effect to directives. In other words, the Court is prepared to apply the terms of unimplemented directives to the relationships between individuals where this can be achieved by implication. The elaboration of this principle, in many respects, ends the distinction between regulations and directives, but at the moment the actual effects and impact of the Court's decision is not yet clear and requires further elaboration from the Court itself.

As regards the proposed amendment of article 189, the following suggestions can be made in the light of this background. First, the text of the article should remain unchanged except for the terms referring to directives. This provision should be altered by the addition of further clauses ensuring that unimplemented directives can be relied upon by private individuals as either grounds for action or as a defence to civil actions or prosecution, but only against the state. The requirements for giving effect to such directives should be clearly stated.

In addition, the organs and public bodies that are considered to be emanations of the state should be defined in order to allow limits to be drawn on the principle. There should also be provision prohibiting Member States from relying on unimplemented directives against individuals: see *Officier van Justitie* v *Kolpinghuis Nijmegen BV* (7).

References

(1) [1989] 2 WLR 997
(2) [1979] ECR 419
(3) [1970] ECR 825
(4) [1986] ECR 723
(5) [1984] ECR 1891
(6) [1992] 1 CMLR 305
(7) [1989] 2 CMLR 18

QUESTION 3

General Comment

A question dealing with two separate areas of Community law but both concerning trade in goods. To answer the question, it is necessary to compare and contrast the policy reasons behind Community competition law with the principle of the free movement of goods.

Skeleton Solution

Purposes of European competition law and policy.

Relationship between article 85 and the provisions relating to the free movement of goods.

Decision of the ECJ in *Consten & Grundig*.

Limitations applying to the relationship.

Suggested Solution

Article 85 of the EEC Treaty prohibits all agreements, decisions and concerted practices between commercial enterprises if they affect trade between Member States and have, as their object or effect, the prevention, restriction or distortion of competition within the Community. Together with article 86, this provision forms the basis of the competition policy of the Community.

The purpose of article 85 is relatively straightforward; it is intended to prevent commercial parties erecting barriers to trade between Member States by means of private agreements or contracts. For example, if a British company and a German company are both engaged in the production or supply of the same goods and agree not to sell their products in the national market of the other party, goods would not flow from Germany to the United Kingdom and vice versa. In the absence of competition both companies could set their prices in their respective markets without reference to the prices charged by the other. This would undoubtedly have the effect of depriving consumers of lower prices which generally result from competition between producers and supplies.

Agreements fixing prices, controlling or limiting production, or permitting price discrimination are potentially anti-competitive because they prevent or restrict distortion. Each of these arrangements impedes the normal free flow of goods by erecting artificial barriers to trade.

There is little doubt that, at least theoretically, competition policy and the principle of the free movement of goods are related because both seek to reduce barriers to trade within the Community.

It will be recalled that article 8A of the EC Treaty introduced the concept of an internal market, defined as an area 'without internal frontiers in which the free movement of goods ... is ensured'. Article 12 prohibits customs duties and any charges having equivalent effect on the flow of goods between Member States while articles 30 and 34 prevent the imposition of quantitative restrictions and measures having an equivalent effect on imports between Member States.

These are measures taken by the relevant national authorities of each Member State for particular purposes. These rules, and the objective which they seek to achieve, namely the free movement of goods, would be circumvented if private parties were allowed to substitute private barriers to prevent effective competition and the free movement of goods. The decision of the European Court in *Consten & Grundig* v *EC Commission* (1) supports this view.

In this case, Grundig, a German manufacturer of electrical equipment, entered into a distribution agreement with Consten, a French distributor. This agreement appointed Consten as Grundig's exclusive agent in certain regions of France. However, a French competitor imported Grundig's products, in free circulation in Germany, into France where they were sold at prices beneath those being offered by Consten.

Consten brought an action in the French courts to prevent its rival from importing in this manner, but the European Commission objected to this procedure and commenced an investigation into the commercial activities of Consten. The Commission found that the distribution agreement was contrary to article 85(1) because the agreement had the effect of distorting competition in the Community because it restricted trade. Both parties brought an action against the Commission in the European Court to have this decision annulled.

The Court held that an agreement could only be contrary to article 85(1) if it affected trade between Member States. It is only to the extent that an agreement affects trade between Member States that the deterioration in competition caused by the agreement falls within article 85; otherwise it would escape the prohibitions contained in article 85(1).

To assess whether an agreement affects trade between Member States, it is necessary to assess whether an agreement is capable of constituting a threat, either direct or indirect, actual or potential, to the free movement of goods between Member States in a manner which might harm the attainment of the objectives of a single market among the Member States. In other words, the degree to which an agreement affects trade between Member States is determined by reference to the amount of distortion it causes to the achievement of the free movement of goods.

If commercial agreements do not impede the free flow of goods from Member States, they do not fall within the scope of article 85(1). But, for this condition to be satisfied, it is not necessary that there is actual trade between parties situated in different countries. In the past, the Commission and the Court have held that agreements between two or more parties in the same Member State may be anti-competitive even though there is no element of transnational trade. For example, in *Cementhandeleren* v *EC Commission* (2), the Court held that a price fixing cartel between cement manufacturers in the Netherlands was contrary to article 85 even though no participant was from outside the Netherlands, simply because the effect of the cartel inside the Netherlands prevented or impeded imports from other Member States.

Similarly, in *Stergios Delimitis* v *Henninger Bräu* (3), the Court held that an exclusive supply agreement between a bar owner and a brewery was contrary to article 85(1) even though both parties conducted business in Germany because of the cumulative effect of similar agreements between the brewery and various third parties.

The degree to which competition law and the principle of the free movement of goods complement each other is also evidenced by the fact that the operation of both is primarily in the interest of the consumer. Naturally, it is in the interests of the consumer that no customs duties, quantitative restrictions or measures having an equivalent effect are imposed on goods since these would merely increase the final price or limit the choice of goods available to consumers. Competition between producers and suppliers also has the overall effect of lowering average prices.

However, while the relationship between article 85 and the principle of the free movement of goods is certainly tangible, it may be going too far to suggest that article 85 is intended only to support the rules for the free movement of goods. The purpose of article 85 is wider than mere support for the principle of the free movement of goods. It provides a comprehensive framework for the operation of an effective Community policy on competition.

The purpose of competition policy in a market economy is more than merely protecting consumer interests. It is intended to promote efficiency by allowing businesses to compete with each other, generally on fair terms and without one or the other having an unfair competitive advantage. It would be grossly unfair, for example, for a number of businesses to group together and pool their resources merely for the purposes of eliminating a competitor from the market.

The EC Commission itself has observed that articles 85 and 86 are intended to provide a commercial environment where competition is not distorted: *EEC Competition Policy in the Single Market* (2nd ed, 1989). In other words, competition policy provides a level playing field throughout the Community where companies can compete in the knowledge that their competitors are subject to similar commercial and trading conditions.

Further, article 85 applies not only to goods, but also to the supply of services. It is therefore equally applicable to the freedom to provide services as it is to the free movement of goods. In the past, for example, banking services have been the subject of investigation by the Commission: see *Zuchner* v *Bayerische Vereinsbank* (4). Similarly, in *Ahmed Saeed Flugreisen* v *Zentrale Zur Bekämpfung* (5), the economic activity under review was the supply of airline services. So, there is no logical restriction of article 85 to its relationship with the principle of the free movement of goods.

References

(1) [1966] ECR 299
(2) [1972] ECR 977
(3) Case 234/89, Judgment of 28 February 1991
(4) [1981] ECR 2021
(5) [1990] 4 CMLR 102

QUESTION 4

General Comment

This is a straightforward question in which students are required to provide a detailed description of the European Commission's role in the constitutional structure of the Community. Relatively high marks may be scored in the event that the student has a grasp of the basic elements of this part of the syllabus because of the general nature of the question.

Skeleton Solution

The constitutional position of the Commission in the instructional structure of the Community.

Powers: supervisory functions, initiation of policy, protection of the interests of the Community, exercise of powers conferred by both treaties and legislation.

Factors influencing the role of the Commission since 1958.

Additional powers and functions exercised by the Commission today.

Suggested Solution

The European Commission plays an orchestrating role within the Community in the formulation of Community legislation and policy. While it performs its functions in conjunction with other Community institutions, particularly the Council of Ministers and the European Parliament, the Commission is ultimately responsible for the initiation of policy and legislative proposals.

Without the Commission, no Community legislation would be enacted, no international negotiations entered into with other countries, and there would be considerably fewer instances of Member States being brought before the European Court for infringements of Community law. While the Council of Ministers represents the interests of the Member States and the European Parliament the interests of the peoples of Europe in the running of the Community, the Commission is the embodiment of the Community interests in the process. Ultimately, it is the European Commission that has responsibility to ensure that the interests of the Community are fully protected, particularly as against the Member States.

Originally the Commission was given four functions under article 155 of the EEC Treaty.

First, the Commission is required to ensure respect for the rights and obligations imposed on both Member States and Community institutions by the Community Treaties and Community legislation. Acting under this authority, the Commission regularly institutes proceedings against Member States alleged to have violated Community obligations (article 169 EEC Treaty) and against Community institutions considered to have acted outside the scope of their powers (article 173 EEC Treaty).

Second, the Commission has been given charge of formulating, initiating and participating in the policy making process within the Community. It is this function that gives the Commission much of its power within the legislative process. While the Council of Ministers is the organ which eventually approves legislative proposals, the Commission has considerable discretion as regards the shaping and content of those proposals. It is true that both the Council of Ministers and the European Parliament are able to suggest amendments to proposals but, ultimately, without the drafting of proposed measures no policies would ever be formulated and no legislative measures ever enacted.

Third, it is required to promote the interests of the Community inside and outside the Community with regard to relations with other countries. Thus, the Commission is permitted to conduct negotiations with third parties on matters that fall within the scope of the Community's competence as defined in the constitutional treaties.

Finally, the Commission is instructed to exercise the powers delegated to it by the Council for the implementation and administration of Community policy. For example, the Commission has extensive powers as regards the enforcement of Community competition policy. It can enact decisions requiring private companies and firms to desist from certain anti-competitive practices and can impose fines subject to review by the European Court.

The functions and powers of the Commission were not substantially altered by the Merger Treaty in 1967. This agreement merely consolidated the functions and powers of the Commission in one single source.

The same cannot be said of the Single European Act (SEA) negotiated in 1986 which significantly amended the EEC Treaty. This agreement in fact had three separate effects on the powers of the Commission. Firstly, the treaty altered the relationship between the Commission and the European Parliament in the legislative process as far as legislation on certain subjects was concerned. Secondly, the Act gave greater competencies to the Community in certain areas of policy. Since the Commission is in charge of the formulation of policy, any growth in the responsibilities of the Community necessarily entails a greater amount of power in the hands of the Commission. Thirdly, the role of the Commission in the external affairs of the Community was greatly enhanced through recognition of the institutional status of the European Council.

Prior to 1986, the role of the European Parliament in the legislative process was restricted to a consultative role except for certain measures which required the consent of Parliament for approval, such as the approval of the budget. The SEA altered this function by establishing the cooperation procedure for legislation of particular subjects such as measures for the creation of the internal market. The Commission consults the European Parliament when formulating proposals for legislation. The Parliament is again given an opportunity to comment on the contents of proposals after the Council of Ministers has approved the draft measure: see *European Parliament* v *EC Council (Re Road Haulage Services)* (1). In effect, this procedure adds a second reading stage to the legislative process which allows the European Parliament a greater say than before.

Obviously, any requirements imposed on the Commission to cooperate, consult or discuss proposed measures with another Community organ tend to dilute its power over the shape and contents of the proposed measure. The more influence Parliament acquired in the legislative process, the less dominance the Commission will be able to exercise. This development has required the Commission to change its role in the Community legislative framework in light of its changing function.

At the same time, the Single European Act considerably extended the areas of competence of the Community. Matters which were previously considered outside the remit of the Community were expressly included within its competence after the 1986 amendments. For example, the Community now has new responsibilities in the fields of consumer protection policy, environmental protection policy, economic cooperation, social policy and research and technological development.

The organic growth in responsibilities within the Community directly affects the powers and duties of the Commission. Essentially, the Commission can assert its competence over all matters falling within the scope of the Community Treaties as amended. As the competence of the Community grows so too does the power and influence of the Commission. In the new areas of responsibility added by the SEA, it is the Commission that has the power to influence the shape and content of these policies simply because it drafts proposals in these areas for consideration in conjunction with the other Community institutions.

The growing external competence of the Commission was also recognised in the Single European Act which acknowledged the institutional status of the European Council. Within the European Council, the Commission is represented by the President of the Commission assisted by another Commissioner. This allows the Commission to influence the discussions, dialogue and negotiations which take place within this organ and which, for the most part, concern issues of foreign policy.

The next major restructuring of the European Community will occur after the Treaty on European Union, signed at Maastricht in February 1992, is ratified by all Member States and comes into force. At the time of writing, the fate of this agreement has not been decided due to the rejection of the text by the Danish population in June, but it has been accepted in referenda in both Ireland and France. It would therefore be superfluous to identify the changes that will be brought by this agreement to the role and function of the Commission except to observe that, as a general proposition, any growth in responsibilities for the Community involves a related growth in the powers of the Commission.

Reference

(1) Case 65/90 (1992) The Times 3 November

QUESTION 5

General Comment

This is an essay-type question requiring a narrative answer. It requires knowledge of the purpose and function of the article 177 procedure as well as insight into the role of article 5 of the EEC Treaty. The essence of the question concerns the ability of the student to assess the degree to which these articles achieve the same goals.

Skeleton Solution

Purposes of article 177; assistance in interpretation and uniform application of Community law.

The pursuit of these objectives through article 177.

Relevance of article 5 EEC Treaty.

Limitations: direct actions; *Francovich* decision.

Suggested Solution

Article 177 of the EEC Treaty allows national courts to refer questions of Community law to the European Court for interpretation and for pronounce-ments on the validity and interpretation of acts of the Community organs. Several conventions negotiated among the Community's Member States, such as the Convention on the Jurisdiction and Enforcement of Judgments 1968, also provide that national courts can refer questions of interpretation to the Court for a ruling.

As the European Court itself pointed out in *CILFIT* v *Ministry of Health* (1), the procedure under article 177 is designed to encourage 'the proper application and uniform interpretation of Community law in all the Member States'. The mechanism establishes a procedure whereby national courts and the European Court can cooperate to ensure that there is little possibility of decisions of national courts on questions of Community law differing from the judgments of the European Court on the same issues.

Thus, the preliminary ruling procedure allows the Court to maintain an element of consistency on both a geographical level and at a jurisprudential level.

However, it should be noted that article 177 does not establish a hierarchy between the European Court and national courts. The preliminary ruling procedure does not mean that the ECJ is a court of final appeal on matters of Community law. Rather, article 177 creates a system whereby national courts and tribunals can seek guidance from the European Court rather than having a decision imposed on them.

An example of this relationship working in practice is the policy of the European Court to only answer questions of Community law. It will not respond to questions of fact or matters requiring an interpretation of national law. In the event that a national court refers a question dealing with points of national law, the European Court merely extracts the relevant points of Community law from the reference before conveying its responses to the national court.

As observed above, the purpose of article 177 is two-fold. First, to ensure the proper application and effectiveness of Community law and, second, to guarantee the uniform interpretation of Community law throughout the Community.

For present purposes, proper application is synonymous with effective enforcement. Article 177 itself assists to ensure this objective by requiring all national courts of final instance seized of a question of Community law to refer the issue to the European Court for interpretation. While not all lower courts are required to make such a reference, this avenue is, of course, open to them should they wish to do so.

The important point is that article 177 envisaged all questions of Community law, at least potentially, being interpreted by the European Court. This scheme would ensure proper and effective enforcement by creating an all-embracing scheme to coordinate the implementation of Community law through the European Court.

However, in certain respects, the European Court has contributed itself to the demise of this system. In *CILFIT* v *Ministry of Health*, the Court, under considerable pressure from national courts, developed the doctrine of acte clair. Courts of final instance would no longer be required to make a mandatory reference if previous decisions of the European Court dealt adequately with the point at issue. In other words, if there was an earlier judgment of the court dealing with similar facts, national courts were released from the obligation to refer.

While it is true that the European Court set down rules for the application of the doctrine of acte clair, at the same time it is clear that it has undermined the effective application of Community law. National courts do not feel themselves under so much pressure to refer questions to the European Court. While this development was largely predictable once Community law had grown into a sizeable corpus of law with the assistance of the Court, nevertheless there are undoubtedly side-effects as regards effective enforcement of Community obligations.

On the other hand, the uniform interpretation of Community law has been achieved by the Court actively encouraging national courts to make preliminary references. For example, the Court will accept virtually all cases referred to it by national courts, no matter how trivial, if there is a genuine dispute.

The only exception to this rule is that the Court will refuse to answer a point of Community law if there is no contentious dispute between the parties. For example, in *Foglia* v *Novello* (2), a reference was made by an Italian court in a dispute between two Italians concerning a sales contract that required delivery of goods in France. The European Court strongly felt that the dispute had been contrived by the parties for the purpose of obtaining a ruling on the consistency of French measures with Community law. The Court also objected to the reference on the ground that it involved a challenge to the sovereign rights of a Member State, ie the right to tax, in a forum in which the state was not in a position to defend itself.

However, this policy of the Court has also had unfortunate and unseen consequences. The present volume of cases was never anticipated and now the average period of delay between the initial reference and a decision on the matter stands at two years. This delay is unacceptable once it is acknowledged that the matter may have been before a national court for some time prior to the reference.

The relationship of article 5 of the EEC Treaty to article 177 is largely a separate issue. Article 177 is a procedure designed to ensure the effective enforcement and uniform application of Community law in national courts. Article 5 is intended to be a substantive obligation imposed on all governmental organs and agencies of Member States to ensure respect for Community law. Thus, while article 177 promotes compliance with Community law by national courts and tribunals, article 5 is a broader obligation imposed on all government organs.

Article 5 has been used extensively by the European Court to keep Member States in line with their Community obligations. For example, this provision forms the basis for the principle of the direct effect of unimplemented directives since the decision of the European Court in *Marleasing SA* v *La Commercial Internacional De Alimentacion SA* (3). In that case, the European Court held that article 5 requires all Member States to take all appropriate measures to ensure the fulfilment of their Community obligations and it follows from this that their national laws must be interpreted to achieve this aim.

The same article also forms the basis for most of the actions brought by the European Commission against Member States for non-implementation of Community regulations and directives: see for example, *EC Commission* v *Belgium (Re Privileges and Immunities of European Community Officials)* (4). Equally, actions brought by the Commission for failure by a Member State to abide by the terms of an adverse ruling in the European Court are brought under this provision and not the article providing grounds for the first offence.

The scope of article 5 is considerable. It applies not only to acts attributable to Member States, but also to their omissions. Thus, in the recent *Francovich case* (5), the Court held that private individuals have a right to sue their own Member States for damages if the Member State acts in a manner contrary to Community law, if the consequences of such actions cause injury to the individual.

While articles 177 and 5 can be seen in the broadest context as complementing each other, their relationship is not an essential one. Both serve to ensure compliance with Community law, one from a procedural perspective, the other from a substantive perspective. They are not, however, interdependent on each other.

References

(1) [1982] ECR 3415
(2) [1980] ECR 745
(3) [1992] 1 CMLR 305
(4) [1989] 2 CMLR 797
(5) (1991) The Times 20 November

QUESTION 6

General Comment

A problem-type question requiring the student to analyse the facts presented in light of articles 30 and 36 of the EC Treaty. There appear to be no real difficulties presented by the facts of the question and so a familiarity with the basic elements of this part of the syllabus should secure a reasonable score.

Skeleton Solution

General principles relating to the free movement of goods.

Restrictions on customs duties and charges having similar effect: article 12.

Restrictions on the use of quantitative restrictions and measures having equivalent effect: articles 30 and 36.

Exemptions for Member States from the rigours of harmonising legislation under article 100A.

Suggested Solution

There are three separate measures preventing Martin NV from importing the aerials from the Netherlands into the United Kingdom: inspection charges; consumer protection legislation; and product technical standards. While each of these measures constitutes a barrier to trade in terms of the free movement of goods, each is subject to different Community rules. It is therefore necessary to consider each measure separately.

Article 12 of the EEC Treaty expressly prohibits the introduction of any customs duties, or charges having an equivalent effect to customs duties, on imports and exports from different Member States of the Community. This provision has been given direct effect by the European Court and may therefore be founded upon by private individuals in national courts without reference to the European Court.

Charges having equivalent effect to customs duties have been defined by the European Court as 'any pecuniary charge, whatever its designation and mode of application, which is imposed unilaterally on goods by reason of the fact that they cross a frontier, and is not a customs duty in the strict sense'; *EC Commission* v *Germany (Re Inspection Fees)* (1). A charge imposed on importation which has the effect of discriminating between domestic goods and similar goods of Community origin, and which cannot be justified by provisions in the EEC Treaty or Community legislation, will therefore amount to a charge having equivalent effect.

Charges having an equivalent effect can only be justified in three circumstances: (a) if the charges relate to a general system of internal levies applied systematically within a Member State and without discrimination; (b) if the charges constitute payment for a service in fact rendered and are in proportion to the costs of receiving that service; and (c) if the charges are levied under the authority of a Community measure harmonising customs procedures.

According to the facts of this case as presented in the question, UK law requires inspection of these products at the port of entry and a charge is due for such an inspection. It is unlikely that such inspections are made of domestically-produced aerials and there is therefore a presumption that such charges are unlawful under Community law. Further, although the charge imposed was for a service rendered, in the event that this charge is disproportionate to the costs of rendering the service, again the charge may be illegitimate.

Further, no direct benefit accrued to either Martin NV or Nairn Ltd by virtue of the inspection. Community law requires that the importer receives some benefit from the service which has not happened in this case. Obviously a direct benefit will not accrue to an importer if the charges are made in the interests of the inspecting state: *EC Commission* v *Italy (Re Customs Administrative Charges)* (2).

In these circumstances, it is unlikely that Martin or Nairn will be liable for the charges and the appropriate action can be raised on these grounds to reject such a claim.

The second barrier to import is the fact that the aerials are made of an aluminium alloy prohibited under United Kingdom consumer protection legislation.

Article 30 of the EEC Treaty prohibits quantitative restrictions on imports along with all measures having an equivalent effect to quantitative restrictions. Measures having an equivalent effect to quantitative restrictions have been defined as 'all trading rules enacted by Member States which are capable of hindering directly or indirectly, actually or potentially, intra-Community trade': *Procureur du Roi* v *Dassonville* (3). All rules enacted by a Member State to regulate trade, and which have the effect of hindering commerce, may contravene article 30 unless they can benefit from an exception to this rule.

In the *Cassis de Dijon* case (4), the European Court considered the question of national restrictions affecting the free movement of goods. It concluded that, in the absence of Community-wide measures of harmonisation, Member States retain authority to enact laws and regulations in relation to products but only so far as such provisions are necessary to satisfy 'mandatory requirements' and the defence of the consumer. However, such measures cannot be discretionary, disproportionate to the objectives which they seek to achieve, or in conflict with Community law.

At the same time, there is a presumption that if goods satisfy the safety standards established in one Member State, they will satisfy the counterpart standards in other Member States.

The first question is whether the measure constitutes a disguised form of discrimination. This is unlikely because the alloy is prohibited from being used in the manufacture of similar products within the United Kingdom.

Whether the measure is disproportionately excessive in relation to the object which it seeks to achieve depends largely on the quality of the material. If it is inherently dangerous or toxic an absolute ban on its use is not disproportionate. If, however, scientific evidence does not support the theory that the material is dangerous, it is far less likely that such an absolute ban could be justified.

There is no suggestion that the material is the subject of regulation at the Community level and we must therefore presume that the prohibition on use is not contrary to Community law.

In the event that the prohibition does not satisfy these conditions, the British authorities may rely on article 36 of the EEC Treaty which allows measures designed to ensure the protection of the health and lives of humans. Naturally, however, in order to rely on this provision, the United Kingdom would have to establish that the material presents a genuine threat to the health of the general population.

The final measure preventing importation is the technical standards relating to the strength of the aerials.

From the facts presented, it appears that Community-wide measures have been adopted to harmonise these standards otherwise the United Kingdom could not have made use of the article 100A exception.

Article 100A provides that a Member State may derogate from the application of a harmonisation measure enacted to secure the internal market so long as the justification for the derogation can be based on either the terms of article 36 or on the ground that it relates to the protection of the environment or working conditions.

If the United Kingdom has secured such a derogation, the exception will be legitimately based on one of these grounds.

However, derogations must be notified to the Commission and if this has not been properly done the exception cannot be relied upon by the British government. It must therefore be verified that the appropriate procedures have been complied with by the United Kingdom.

The second ground which may be founded upon by Martin stems from the fact that often such derogations are of a temporary nature. In other words, Member States are allowed to rely on the derogation only for a particular period. If the period of authorisation has expired, the derogation will no longer be valid and the measures cannot be justified.

References

(1) [1990] 1 CMLR 561
(2) [1989] 1 CMLR 213
(3) [1974] ECR 837
(4) [1979] ECR 649

QUESTION 7

General Comment

A popular question requiring consideration of the implications of the right of establishment for the legal profession.

Skeleton Solution

The complexities of the existing legal position.

The primary legislation.

Case law and precedents.

Council Directive 89/48 (1989).

Suggested Solution

It is not yet possible to make a categorical statement that once a person is qualified to practise law in one Community Member State, he or she may practise law in another Member State. This lack of clarity is mainly due to the uncertain scope of article 52 of the EEC Treaty which creates the right of establishment and article 59 which regulates the right to provide services and appears to imply a more temporary arrangement. The European Court has, however, stressed the parallels between article 48 (free movement of workers, on the one hand and articles 52 and 59 on the other hand. Specifically, the Court has observed that the three articles comprise 'an integrated whole': *Procureur du Roi* v *Royer* (1).

Council Directive 77/249 (1977) was designed to clarify this matter. It is concerned with the recognition of a lawyer coming from another Member State as a lawyer who intends to offer his legal services in that state. It is therefore only concerned with the freedom to provide services (although it has been introduced on the basis of articles 57 and 66 of the EEC Treaty) and has no effect on the right of establishment in a host state with all the consequent benefits for the immigrant's family. This would require an additional step, namely the mutual recognition of qualifications which has not yet been achieved (in contrast see Directives 75/362 and 75/363 on the mutual recognition of medical qualifications).

A lawyer is permitted to practise in another Member State under the directive but this freedom is subject to various conditions. First, under article 4(1), representation of a client in legal proceedings or before public authorities in a Member State must be carried out under the conditions laid down for lawyers established in that legal system, but there are exceptions to restrict certain types of common restrictions such as residence qualifications and the need to register with any professional body.

Article 5 of the directive permits supplementary conditions to be imposed on the foreign lawyer with respect to supervision in procedural matters. Since actual appearance before a foreign court is likely to be hampered by linguistic difficulties, the directive authorises the state to introduce a supervision requirement which means that a lawyer fully qualified in that jurisdiction must be present at any hearing. Also, when giving legal advice, certain basic rules of the host state can be imposed on foreign lawyers in addition to the professional rules of the Member State concerned; article 4(4). Finally, a foreign lawyer may be excluded from making wills in the host country and can be refused the right to represent an employer if he is salaried in-house counsel; article 6.

The influence of this directive has been supplemented by the development of a considerable body of jurisprudence by the European Court. The policy of the Court has been to try to offer greater freedom to the foreign lawyer. In *Reyners* v *Belgian State* (2), the leading case in this area, a Dutch national resident in Belgium relied upon article 52 in order to challenge a nationality requirement for entry to the bar. The plaintiff in question was born in Belgium, educated there, and had taken his Docteur en Droit Belge, only to be refused admission to the Belgian bar because of his Dutch nationality.

The European Court held that the prohibition of discrimination contained in article 52 of the EEC Treaty, concerning the right of establishment, was directly applicable and could be relied on by the plaintiff to found directly enforceable rights. The Court continued to find that the objective of article 52 was to be achieved by the Council of Ministers through a legislative programme, but the direct effect of the provision did not depend on the initiation of such a programme.

The Court went one stage further in *Thieffery* v *Paris Bar Council* (3). This case demonstrated that, even in the absence of rights under article 57, recognition of foreign legal qualifications may be compelled under article 52 which prohibits discrimination on the grounds of nationality. Thieffery, a Belgian national, held a Belgian degree recognised by the University of Paris as equivalent to a French law degree. He also acquired the qualifying certificate for the profession of advocate as required by the Bar Council.

However, the Paris Bar Council refused to allow him to undergo practical training because he did not possess a French law degree. The European Court rejected this contention and held that, if the qualification was recognised as equivalent its French counterpart, article 52 did not allow discrimination to the perpetrated merely because the qualifications had been granted in separate countries.

The next case, *Ordre des Advocats* v *Klopp* (4), appears to have had the effect of placing foreign lawyers in a better position to practise than national lawyers. Article 52 et seq of the EEC Treaty were held by the Court to preclude the denial of a national from one Member State of the right to enter and thereafter to practise the profession of advocate solely on the ground that he maintains chambers in another Member State. This was despite the fact that national lawyers were prevented by the Bar rules from maintaining more than one set of chambers within the national territory.

The host state's rules of professional conduct apply to all foreign lawyers practising within the state, provided these rules do not discriminate between national and foreign lawyers: *Gulleng* v *Ordre des Advocats* (5).

Directly applicable rights derived from article 52 assist foreign lawyers secure a greater degree of freedom to practise while mitigating the defects arising from the operation of the directive. Naturally, the permitted derogations from article 52 are also applicable to the freedom of establishment of lawyers.

Article 55 allows Member States to deviate from the application of article 52 for the appointment of persons to official positions. For example, a number of the duties of notaries public may be deemed to fall within this category and, in the *Reyners* case, above, the European Court was asked whether the 'official authority exception' could be used to allow discrimination in the appointment of lawyers who also act as notaries public. The Court, while tacitly acknowledging that the occasional exercise of such functions may be considered an exercise of official authority, declared that this was not the case with respect to the advocate's other responsibilities. The state therefore could not rely on article 55.

As part of the single internal market programme, Council Directive 89/48 (1989) was enacted to establish a general system for the mutual recognition of higher education diplomas. This directive supplants the earlier one and provides that, after 1 January 1991, lawyers qualified in the United Kingdom and in the rest of the Community will, in principle, be able to practice anywhere in the Community provided they have obtained a degree or diploma following a minimum of at least three years' university education, and also completed relevant professional training or have acquired some relevant professional experience in their country of qualification or the host country.

The directive permits a number of derogations to be made to this basic principle in the event that there are major differences between the legal education and training received by the migrant lawyer and that received by lawyers qualified in the intended host country. In such cases 'compensatory mechanisms' can be introduced. These allow Member States to introduce safeguards to ensure minimum standards of legal counsel. These mechanisms include the introduction of aptitude tests and the use of probationary supervision periods, extending to a maximum of three years' duration during which the foreign lawyer is supervised by a qualified lawyer.

The types of compensatory mechanism that are appropriate for the purposes of converting experience are at the discretion of the Member States, but such measures cannot be more restrictive than necessary to achieve the legitimate objectives of the legislation. Thus, for example, in *EC Commission* v *Germany (Re Restrictions on the Legal Profession)* (6), the European Court held that German restrictions preventing foreign lawyers from visiting persons in custody unless accompanied by a German lawyer were unlawful on the basis that these restrictions went further than necessary to achieve the objective of protecting the public from unqualified and inexperienced foreign lawyers.

References

(1) [1976] ECR 497
(2) [1974] ECR 631
(3) [1976] ECR 765
(4) [1985] 1 CMLR 99
(5) [1988] 2 CMLR 57
(6) [1989] 2 CMLR 677

QUESTION 8

General Comment

An essay-type question requiring a narrative answer on the subject of the internal market programme. The question has three distinct parts and the answer must address each of these aspects of the question individually.

Skeleton Solution

Legal basis for the internal market programme: article 8A.

Fundamental principles of the programme.

Legislative procedures for the enactment of appropriate legislation.

Suggested improvements to the existing process.

Suggested Solution

The Single European Act 1986 introduced a number of new policy objectives for the European Community by amending the EC Treaty. Of these, one of the most significant and successful was the initiation of a programme designed to create a single internal market. Article 8A of the EC Treaty, as amended, defines the internal market as 'an area without internal frontiers in which the free movement of goods, persons, services and capital is ensured in accordance with the provisions of the [EC Treaty]'. The deadline for the achievement of this goal has been set as 31 December 1992.

The internal market programme is designed to eliminate or reduce all major physical, technical and fiscal barriers to trade thereby attaining free movement of goods, persons, services and capital. The programme entails an extensive legislative agenda harmonising national legal provisions relating to customs procedures, taxation, public procurement, capital movements, company law, intellectual property, employment and investment. These measures are required because the existing disparities between each of the Member States in these areas impede the creation of a harmonious and consistent environment for the production and sale of goods and the conduct of commerce.

Within the Community, physical barriers to the free flow of goods presently exist for many reasons such as to enforce national quotas for certain products, to collect VAT and excise duties, to carry out health inspections and checks, to operate the Community system of compensation under the Common Agricultural Policy, to ensure compliance with transportation regulations and to collect statistical information.

To reduce the effect of these barriers and to facilitate the free movement of goods, simplified customs procedures have been adopted. The adoption of the Single Administrative Document (SAD) is intended to reduce delays caused by the multiple processing of customs forms. The introduction of common border posts (banalisation) where all formalities are confined to a single stopping point between each Member State has been introduced to pave the way for the eventual removal of all systematic controls at frontiers.

It is the existence of technical barriers to the construction of the internal market that causes the greatest problems. These barriers result in standards and conditions which retard the practical exercise of the four freedoms. Technical barriers to trade in goods include the diversity of national regulations and standards for testing products or for the protection and safety of the consumer, the duplication of product testing and certification requirements (such as exist in the pharmaceutical industry) and the reluctance of public authorities to open their procurement contracts to the nationals of other Member States.

There are two fundamental legal principles behind the elimination of the technical barrier to the proper functioning of the free movement of goods. These are the principle of equivalence and the principle of harmonisation.

The principle of equivalence or mutual recognition requires that, once a product has been manufactured in one Member State, it is capable of being sold without restrictions throughout the Community. In other words, if a product meets the technical or safety standards of one Member State, there is a presumption that it will meet the counterpart requirements in other Members. The use of this principle was sanctioned in the *Cassis de Dijon* case (1) and was also reiterated in the *German Beer Purity* case (2).

The second principle is that of harmonisation. This requires that measures standardising technical and safety requirements within the Community are adopted at the Community level. Generally, this requires the passing of Community legislation. The SEA ensures that legislation for this purpose will receive expedited passage by lowering the voting requirements in the Council of Ministers to enacting such measures to majority voting.

Where harmonising legislation is not absolutely required, the Commission has expressed its intention to rely on the principle of equivalence as applied by the European Court to attack remaining barriers. A substantial amount of Community legislation pertaining to the harmonisation of technical standards, mostly in the form of directives, has been passed to approximate technical standards on products.

Failure to achieve the four freedoms before the Single European Act was widely attributed to the legislative process which existed within the Community prior to 1986. In order to realise the achievement of these four goals, it was necessary to liberate the legislative process from the stranglehold of the requirement for unanimity among all Member States. Article 100A of the EC Treaty, as amended, introduced qualified majority voting for all proposed legislation enacted to secure the internal market. Measures enacted under article 100A are designed to approximate or harmonise national measures relating to technical barriers to trade.

Measures designed to tackle the problem of fiscal barriers and proposals relating to the free movement of persons or the rights and interests of employed persons are specifically excluded from the scope of article 100A. Adoption of measures relating to these subjects will continue to require unanimity under article 100 of the EC Treaty. Further, article 100A(4) of the Treaty allows a Member State to derogate from measures enacted on a majority vote if the measure is alleged to adversely affect the security or welfare of that Member State.

At the same time, measures enacted under article 100A are subject to the cooperation procedure which requires that the Commission fully consult the European Parliament as regards proposed legislation. The cooperation procedure adds a second reading stage for certain types of proposed legislation. Under the cooperation procedure, responsibility for the initiation of proposals continues to reside in the European Commission which formulates proposals taking into account the views of the European Parliament, before submitting the proposals to the Council of Ministers for approval.

The Council of Ministers is then required to reach a 'common position' on the measure acting by majority voting. The common position is referred to the European Parliament which can approve the Council position, reject the position, or amend the Council's position. If the position is amended, the Commission has one month to consider the amendments proposed by Parliament with a view to taking these into account when amending its proposal.

There is little doubt that the amended legislation procedure has contributed significantly to the passage of legislation to create a single internal market. Member States can no longer veto such measures because the requirement of unanimity has been removed. Similarly, the European Parliament has made a significant contribution to the content of proposed legislation.

Yet, at the same time, the creation of the article 100A process has opened the door to potential abuse of the legislative process. Thus, frequently Member States and the Commission clash on the legitimate basis for a particular measure. Naturally, if a measure is based on a provision of the Treaty that requires unanimity, it is easy for the Commission to assert that the proper legal basis for the measures is Article 100A and thereby substitute majority voting for unanimity.

For example, the European Commission suggested that the controversial Fifth Company Directive on the Statute for European Companies could be enacted by means of article 100A and not article 100 as originally proposed. The difference was that unanimity was required under article 100 but qualified voting applied to measures processed through article 100A. The United Kingdom government threatened to take this matter to the European Court if the European Commission tried to follow this route. Eventually, the European Commission withdrew its proposals on this matter.

Legislation is a potent means of achieving European economic integration. Community regulations and directives can effectively harmonise whole areas of national laws. However, their are limits to the effectiveness of legislation. For example, Community legislation must rest on some form of political consensus within the Community that the measure is necessary and appropriate. Often there is a feeling that the European Commission is too far ahead of this political consensus in its proposals. The result is conflict among the Member States and the Community institutions.

At the same time, the creation of a single market will not, by itself, significantly advance the cause of European economic integration. This is clear because the concept of the internal market is considerably more refined than that of a common market which in turn is significantly looser than a European union of states. The internal market programme concentrates on achieving the basic goals of the free movement of goods, labour, services and capital. This reflects a desire on the part of the Member States to achieve at least a bare minimum level of economic integration to sustain the momentum towards true economic, political and monetary union among the Member States.

Action is required in other fields such as social policy, cultural relations, and social interaction. This implies that a number of important political decisions must be made. Political and monetary union can only occur when there is a sufficient degree of economic and social integration among the peoples of Europe. The rejection of the Maastricht Treaty on European Union by Denmark in June 1992 is a signal that the degree of economic and social integration is not yet present to advance the Community towards such a union.

References

(1) [1979] ECR 649
(2) [1988] ECR 1

UNIVERSITY OF LONDON
LLB EXAMINATIONS 1993
for External Students
PARTS I AND II EXAMINATIONS (Scheme A) and THIRD AND FOURTH YEAR EXAMINATIONS (Scheme B)

EC LAW

Wednesday, 16 June: 10.00 am to 1.00 pm

Answer *FOUR* of the following EIGHT questions

1 'The choice of legal basis is a highly controversial, political matter'. What are the guiding principles governing the choice of legal basis? Illustrate your answer with reference to recent case law.

2 What is the role of the European Parliament in the institutional balance of the European Community? How has it developed since the inception of the Community and how might it develop in the future?

3 How and when can conflicts arise between rules of national law and rules of Community law? How should such conflicts be resolved in the view of the European Court of Justice? Discuss with reference to ECJ caselaw.

4 'To give what is called 'horizontal effect' to directives would totally blur the distinction between regulations and directives which the Treaty establishes in Articles 189 and 191' (Advocate General Slynn in Case 152/84 *Marshall* v *Southampton and South-West Hampshire Area Health Authority).*

Discuss.

5 Fruit Ltd, an English company, has developed a fruit called Peach Delight, which is a cross between a peach and an apricot. It has become extremely popular in shops and supermarkets. Foreign rivals have also developed the Peach Delight, but Fruit Ltd still retains a 48 per cent share of the total Peach Delight market in the European Community, although this only constitutes a five per cent share of the total market for fresh fruit.

Fruit Ltd only supplies its Peach Delight to shops which agree to sell only Peach Delight and no other soft fruit. It also insists on charging retailers 75p per Peach Delight. (Production and cultivation costs amount to only 5p per fruit).

a) The European Commission have started an investigation into Fruit Ltd's activities. Advise Fruit Ltd as to how Community law might affect its conditions of sale.

b) Pete Robinson, a small Surbiton grocer, wishes to stock Peach Delight. However, Fruit Ltd has refused to supply him with the fruit because he refuses to comply with Fruit Ltd's conditions. Mr Robinson asks for your advice on the relevant position in European Community law.

6 Consider the following from the point of view of Community law:

a) legislation by a Member State imposing a financial levy on all books published in a foreign language published within or imported into the country.

b) legislation by a Member State requiring all novels sold in the country to state on the title page the nationality of the author;

AND

c) legislation by a Member State banning the sale of all alcoholic drinks but permitting freely their manufacture in private households.

7 Kirsten, a Danish national with a degree in civil engineering, seeks employment in Italy. She is offered a part-time job with Verona City Council. Kirsten is informed by her lawyer that she is not eligible for that job because under the current Italian law the City Council may employ only Italian nationals, since the job is considered to be in the public service. She is also told that her rate of pay would be lower than that paid to full time city engineers and that she would have to retire at the age of 55 while the male civil engineers retire at the age of 60.

Advise Kirsten on the relevant points of Community law.

8 To what extent will Article 171(2) of the draft Treaty on European Union ('Maastricht') and the judgment of the European Court of Justice in *Francovich* resolve the problems surrounding the enforcement of Community law in the Member States by the Commission and for the benefit of individuals?

QUESTION 1

General Comment

The question requires an examination of the principles behind the selection of the most appropriate basis for adopting Community measures. There is ample case law from the court in this connection which candidates are invited to use to illustrate the relevant principles. The subject of the question is relatively unusual although the number of cases presently being brought before the ECJ on this point has recently significantly increased. Possibly this provides the background to the origin of the question.

Skeleton Solution

The proper choice of legal basis: voting requirements, consultations and procedure.

The case law regulating legal principles applicable to the selection of the legal basis.

The sanctions for exceeding the legitimate basis for adopting measures.

The growing influence of the European Parliament.

Suggested Solution

All regulations, directives and decisions of the Council, and the Commission for that matter, must state the legal basis on which they were enacted, the reasons why the measures were required and also reference must be made to any proposals or opinions which were required prior to their adoption; Article 190 EC Treaty. But, in any event, all acts of Community institutions must have a legal basis in the EC Treaty and, in the absence of a proper basis, such acts would be ultra vires.

The most important aspect of selecting the proper legal basis for a measure is that this choice determines the necessary procedural requirements including the necessary vote required in the Council of Ministers for the adoption of the measure, the degree of consultations required between the Council and the European Parliament and the decision-making processes which must be followed for the measure to be approved.

Voting requirements vary not according to the nature of the measure – a regulation, a directive or a decision – but rather according to the subject-matter which the measure is intended to regulate. Article 148(1) of the EC Treaty specifies the general rule that, save as otherwise provided, the Council shall act by a majority of its members. But, in fact, the original EEC Treaty required a unanimous vote for the adoption of most measures which resulted in a mere trickle of legislation being approved.

The EC Treaty was significantly amended in 1986 by the ratification of the Single European Act which introduced majority voting into many more areas of Community competence. Much of the legislation adopted in pursuit of the single internal market programme, for example, was adopted on the basis of Article 100A of the Treaty which authorises majority voting for harmonising measures designed to complete the internal market.

At the other extreme, many areas still require a unanimous vote. Under Article 235, if action by the Community should prove necessary to the attainment of the objectives set out in the Treaty, but the Treaty has not provided the required powers, the Council may adopt the appropriate measures but only by means of a unanimous vote.

The voting criteria required for the adoption of a measure will, of course, significantly affect the nature and content of the final measure. Where unanimity is required, a single Member State may delay the adoption of a measure indefinitely. This has the effect of frustrating negotiations even when the other 11 Member States are in unison.

The United Kingdom, for example, has blocked the adoption of the proposal for a draft statute for the creation of a new legal persona known as 'the European company'. The UK government argues that the appropriate legal basis of the measure is Article 235 while the other Member States claim that Article 100A is a perfectly adequate legal basis. Article 235 requires unanimity while Article 100A merely requires a qualified majority. The UK has used its own legal interpretation to demand significant amendments to the proposal to limit the rights of workers to participate in the management of this type of company. Further, the United Kingdom has threatened that if the measure is adopted under Article 100A, it will immediately initiate proceedings to have the European Court review the matter.

So, the legal basis and the voting requirements fundamentally shape the final form of the measure adopted quite simply because the minority of Member States have more ability and influence in the content of the final measure when unanimity is required than when a qualified majority is sufficient.

A substantial number of cases have come to the attention of the European Court for judicial review of the legal basis for the adoption of Community acts. While the selection of the appropriate legal basis is partly a political matter, the choice must be based on proper legal grounds. It is therefore inaccurate to claim that this selection is solely a political, and not a legal, matter. In fact, the European Court has built up a considerable reservoir of legal principles to allow the review of this selection.

First, the Council of Ministers cannot change the legal basis of a measure proposed by the Commission without proper justification. Thus, in *EC Commission* v *EC Council (Re Generalised Tariff Preferences)* (1), the Commission proposed that the adoption of two measures should be based on Article 113 of the EC Treaty which requires a qualified majority. The Council did not state the legal basis on which it finally adopted the measure – opening itself to an additional challenge under Article 190 – but resorted to a unanimous vote which implied that the measure had been adopted under Article 235.

The Commission raised proceedings in the European Court which held that the Council had sufficient authority to adopt the measures under Article 113. Since unanimous voting had been used and not a qualified majority, the defect was not purely formal and therefore the Court declared the measures void.

Second, the choice of the legal basis for the adoption of a measure does not simply depend on the convictions of a Community institution as to the objective being pursued by the measure. The decision to adopt on the basis of a particular provision must be based on 'objective factors' which are amenable to judicial review; *EC Commission* v *EC Council (Re Generalised Tariff Preferences)*, supra.

Third, the previous practice of a Community organ in the adoption of similar measures has no bearing on the future voting practices of that organ. For example, a mere prior practice on the part of the Council cannot justify derogation from the strict requirements of the Treaty as regards legal basis; see *United Kingdom* v *EC Council* (*Re Hormones*) (2).

Fourth, where authority to adopt a measure is split among two or more provisions, the institution exercising the power is required to adopt the measure in order to satisfy all the relevant provisions. Hence, for example, where a measure is being adopted on the basis of two provisions, one requiring unanimity and the other a qualified majority, the measure must be adopted unanimously; see *EC Commission* v *EC Council (Re Harmonised Commodity Descriptions)* (3).

But, the Court will not slavishly nullify a measure simply because a formal defect exists as regards the legal basis. So, for example, the Court will not declare a measure null and void where, although adopted on the incorrect legal basis, the proper legal basis imposes approximately the same procedural requirements.

The second important consequence of the selection of the proper legal basis is that many of the provisions conferring power to adopt measures can only be properly exercised after some form of consultation with the European Parliament. In this respect the Parliament's powers have grown considerably. Initially, Parliament's right to be consulted in the Community legislative and decision-making processes was extremely limited. However, failure to engage in consultations, in those few areas which required consultations, rendered a putative measure void; see *SA Roquette Freres* v *EC Council* (4).

The influence of the Parliament in this process grew considerably after 1986 once the Single European Act was adopted. Now Parliament is fully involved in the framing of legislative proposals especially under the co-operation procedure. Failure to consult the Parliament properly will render any measure adopted null and void if the omission constitutes an infringement of an essential procedural requirement.

The Parliament is now more actively than ever challenging the legal basis for measures adopted by the Council. First in *European Parliament* v *EC Council (Re Tchernobyl)* (5), and more recently in *European Parliament* v *EC Council (Re Students' Rights)* (6), the Parliament has sought judicial review of measures adopted by the Council alleging that the measures in question were enacted by the Council on inappropriate legal grounds.

Finally, the choice of legal basis will also determine the proper internal Community procedure to be followed for the adoption of a particular measure. For example, where a harmonising measure is adopted under Article 100 of the EC Treaty, the non-co-operation procedure is, pending ratification of the Treaty on European Union, applicable and only informal consultations are required with the Council. But, if a measure is adopted under Article 100A the co-operation procedure must be employed. This involves a different series of rights and duties for the

Council and the Parliament, but also for the European Commission which has responsibility for drafting the final measure after the Council and the Parliament have had their say.

References

(1) [1987] ECR 1493
(2) [1988] 2 CMLR 453
(3) [1990] 1 CMLR 457
(4) [1980] ECR 3333
(5) [1992] 1 CMLR 91
(6) [1992] 3 CMLR 281

QUESTION 2

General Comment

This question involves a commonly recurring theme in past examination papers. The examiner is seeking to test knowledge of the institutional balance within the Community with special reference to the role of the European Parliament. This requires a statement of the constitutional balance vis-a-vis the European Parliament and the Council on the one hand and the Parliament and the Commission on the other. Essentially the question itself is relatively straightforward and should pose no problems for the well versed candidate.

Skeleton Solution

Doctrine of the separation of interests and the role of the European Parliament in this process.

The powers of the Parliament over the Commission.

The budgetary powers of the Parliament: the main power exercisable over both organs.

Powers over the Council and the proposed amendments to these powers in the Treaty on European Union.

Suggested Solution

The EC Treaty, as the constitution of the Community, is based on the doctrine of the separation of interests rather than the separation of powers. The Council of Ministers embodies the interests of the Member States while the European Commission represents the fundamental interests of the Community. The role of the European Parliament is to preserve and protect the interests of the peoples of the Community. At present, pending the amendments to the EC Treaty to be made by the Treaty on European Union (Maastricht Treaty), the Parliament is ill-equipped and exercises insufficient authority to carry out this function particularly as regards the Council's activities.

The powers of the European Parliament in the institutional balance of the Community are, paradoxically, aimed at countering the exercise of authority by the European Commission rather than the Council of Ministers. This should not, strictly speaking, be surprising since the EC Treaty was drafted by representatives of the Member States. But, in fact the most constitutional authority within the Community institutional framework is vested in the Council of Ministers. Any further augmentation of powers for the Parliament should therefore be directed against checking the powers of the Council and not the Commission.

At its inception, the European Parliament had a minor role to play in striking the institutional balance within the Community. Its primary authority lay in its power to collectively dismiss the Commission by a motion of censure carried by a two-thirds majority of votes cast if representing a majority of the members of the Parliament; Article 144 EC Treaty.

On occasions motions had been tabled in the Parliament for the censure of the Commission but, to date, none has been successfully carried. In practice this device is considerably less powerful than it might first appear. Individual Commissioners cannot be dismissed by a vote of the Parliament; all the Commissioners must resign. Therefore, such a motion would penalise Commissioners who have not committed any indiscretion. Also, if the whole Commission cabinet was sanctioned, an undesirable vacuum of authority would develop pending the appointment of a new cabinet. The Parliament has no influence in the selection of the new Commissioners who would be selected by the governments of the Member States.

Parliament members are also permitted to put questions to Commission officials which the Commission staff are obliged to answer; Article 140 EC Treaty. Questions may be submitted both orally and in writing. Commission officials may be subject to scrutiny in both the plenary session and committees of the Parliament. This power is part of the watchdog function carried out by the Parliament. Questions may also be asked of the Council, but these have neither the formal authority nor the same degree of compunction as those submitted to the Commission.

In a similar vein, the Commission is also required to submit an annual general report to the Parliament on the subject of the affairs of the Community; Article 143 EC Treaty. This report forms the basis for the annual Parliamentary debate on the affairs of the Community.

One power, which is exercised over the Council as much as the Commission, is the Parliament's role in the budgetary procedure. The Community's budget is, at present, prepared by the Commission and submitted to the Council, but the Parliament may approve or modify the budget depending on the type of expenditure involved; Article 203 of the EC Treaty, as amended.

The Parliament has power to approve all non-compulsory expenditure – administrative and operational expenditure – which accounts for approximately 25–30 per cent of the total budget each year. In other words, the Parliament can modify this aspect of the budget to a considerable degree. But as regards the remainder of the budget – the compulsory expenditure – the power of the Parliament is confined to proposing modifications which are deemed accepted unless the Council rejects these proposals. The vote of the Council in such a matter is by qualified majority.

Ultimately, Parliament has authority to reject the budget as a whole if, acting by a majority of its members and two-thirds of the votes cast, it believes there are 'important reasons' to reject the draft budget; Article 203(8) EC Treaty. In such an event, the Parliament may request that a new budget is submitted to it for approval. In fact, in 1979 the Parliament did reject the draft budget by a vote of 299 votes to 64, with one abstention.

The power to approve the budget is perhaps the main illustration of the Parliament's power to balance the institutional processes within the Community. It is a power that can be equally exercised over the Council and the Commission alike. However, again the power to veto the whole budget is one which the European Parliament must exercise carefully in order not to create havoc within the Community order.

In any event, the Council has constitutional authority to bring the European Parliament before the European Court if it is suspected that the Parliament has itself abused its powers over the budget; see *EC Council* v *European Parliament (Re The Community Budget)* (1).

As stated earlier, Parliament's influence over the Council is finite and takes two main forms: power to approve the admission of new members and limited participation in the legislative processes.

Under Articles 237 and 238 of the EC Treaty, the consent of the Parliament is required for the admission of new members into the Community and for the conclusion of association agreements between the Community and third states. The negotiation of an association agreement is a preliminary step towards membership of the Community. The Parliament can technically veto the decision of the Council on admission and establishing association agreements which is a significant limitation on the Council's authority in this respect.

But, the historical impotence of the Parliament in restraining the actions of the Council is most evident in the legislative processes carried out within the Community. The legislative competence of the Parliament has progressed through three identifiable stages.

The original legislative role of Parliament was primarily

consultative. The Parliament commented on proposals put forward by the Commission before the Council. It had a right to be consulted on certain matters, ie. under Articles 43, 54, 56 and 87 of the EC Treaty, but in practice the Commission frequently consulted the Parliament during the consultative phase of drafting legislation.

This consultative role was circumscribed in two respects. First, the vast majority of measures did not strictly require the views of the Parliament and so the Council could generally ignore its views. Second, unlike the Member States and the Commission, the Parliament was not permitted to bring proceedings in the European Court against the Council under Article 173(1) of the EC Treaty. Hence, Parliament exercised little control over the activities of the Council.

In 1986, the Single European Act altered the constitutional balance of authority in the Community slightly by introducing the co-operation procedure. The use of the co-operation procedure was required to enact legislation in specific subjects and especially the freedom of establishment, working conditions, and certain forms of harmonisation legislation. The co-operation extended the authority of the Parliament over the Council insofar as the Parliament was permitted two opportunities to discuss proposed measures but, as always, ultimate authority to adopt or reject measures resided in the Council of Ministers.

After the passing of the Single European Act, the Parliament was also successful in persuading the European Court to recognise its standing to bring proceedings against the Council. After a series of unsuccessful cases (see *European Parliament* v *EC Council (Re Common Transport Policy)* (2); and *European Parliament* v *EC Council (Re Comitology)* (3)), the Court eventually recognised the standing of the Parliament to act to safeguard its powers under the Treaty as long as the action was raised solely with that objective; see *European Parliament* v *EC Council (Re Tchernobyl)* (4).

The Treaty on European Union consolidates both these advances in the Parliament's authority over the Council. First, a new comprehensive legislative process modelled on the co-operation procedure will be introduced applying to all legislation, not just legislation on particular subjects. This process is to be known as the 'co-decision procedure' and is contained in Article 189б of the amended EC Treaty. Second, Parliament's right to initiate proceedings against the Council of Ministers is formally recognised in an amended Article 173(3) of the EC Treaty.

In the final assessment, while the European Parliament presently exercises considerable supervisory control over the activities of the Commission, the same cannot be said of its relationship with the Council of Ministers. Whether or not the Treaty on European Union will establish the Parliament as an adequate counterweight to the Council can only be assessed once the new provisions in the Treaty on European Union are inserted into the EC Treaty itself.

References

(1) [1986] 3 CMLR 94
(2) [1985] ECR 1513
(3) [1988] ECR 5615
(4) [1992] 1 CMLR 91

QUESTION 3

General Comment

Another straightforward essay-type question requiring a narrative answer. How and when conflicts arise can best be demonstrated through examples showing the circumstances giving rise to such situations. The policy of the European Court towards the issue is clear-cut and presents no obstacle to answering the question. However we are not asked for the views of the national courts which should only be alluded to in passing.

Skeleton Solution

Outline of the measures of Community law on which the European Court has conferred the quality of supremacy.

Types of incompatible national provisions: statutes, judicial decisions, administrative practices – civil and criminal proceedings.

Occasions when conflicts arise: before the ECJ (Article 169 cases and 177 references) and national courts.

Principle of supremacy as elaborated by the ECJ and adopted by the UK courts in *Factortame.*

Suggested Solution

The European Community legal system does not function independently or separately from the legal systems of the 12 Member States. The provisions of the EC Treaty and Community measures often cover the same subject-matters as national legislation. However, none of the Community Treaties contains provisions expressly regulating the issue of supremacy between Community law and national provisions in the inevitable event of conflict.

This inevitability has required the European Court to develop principles to regulate the relationship between inconsistent provisions of Community law and national law. With varying degree of reluctance, the courts of most of the Member States have gradually accepted these principles and have applied them in cases in which conflict arises.

How conflicts can arise

Conflicts between provisions of Community law and those of national law can arise in a number of circumstances. The most obvious is when a state enacts a statute incompatible with a directly enforceable provision of a Community Treaty. Within the United Kingdom, it has been accepted that a UK statute, enacted prior to or after 1972, if inconsistent with a provision of a Community Treaty, cannot prevail over Community provisions; *R* v *Secretary of State, ex parte Factortame* (1).

There is no logical reason why a statute inconsistent with a Community regulation, or the terms of an illegitimately unimplemented directive should be treated any differently. Lord Bridge of Harwich recognised as much when, in rendering the judgment in *Factortame,* supra. In fact, decisions have been forthcoming from the European Court holding that effect must be given to unimplemented directives capable of direct effect in preference to provisions of national law; see *Pubblico Ministero* v *Ratti* (2).

It is not only statutory law which may be incompatible with provisions of Community law. The formal source of national law is irrelevant in the event of inconsistency. Both inconsistent statutory instruments and judicial decisions have been considered by the European Court. Even rules of professional bodies may, in certain circumstances, be held to conflict with measures of Community law; see *R* v *Royal Pharmaceutical Society of Great Britain* (3).

The possibility of conflict exists irrespective of whether the national law has a civil or a criminal character. For example, Community law may offer a defence to a prosecution if the accused can establish that the charges conflict with Community law. For example, in *Procureur du Roi* v *Dassonville* (4), the accused successfully relied on Article 30 of the EC Treaty as a defence to a charge of importing goods without the proper documentation.

Conflicts can even arise between provisions of a country's constitutional law and Community law. Even in these circumstances, the European Court has refused to accept that provisions of national law – even of a constitutional nature –prevail over Community law; see *Internationale Handelsgesellschaft* (5).

The points in time when conflicts arise

As to the time when conflicts between the two different sets of legal principles occur, generally, this is when either the European Court or a national court is required to rule on the application of Community law to a series of facts before it.

The European Court will consider this matter when either an application is made under Article 169 or when the preliminary ruling procedure of Article 177 of the Treaty is invoked by a national court.

In the event that the issue arises when proceedings are initiated against a Member State under Article 169, the Member States in question are required to repeal national legislation held inconsistent with Community law; see *EC Commission* v *United Kingdom (Re Origin Marking Requirements)* (6). The European Commission bears primary responsibility for ensuring that Member States are brought before the European Court on this basis when in its view a conflict arises.

Member States are obliged under Article 5 of the EC Treaty to adhere to the rulings of the European Court and to amend or repeal offending provisions of national law.

The alternative means whereby conflicts come before the European Court is when a preliminary reference is made. Interestingly, the European Court has no jurisdiction under Article 177 to interpret a provision of national law and is therefore unable to declare a particular national statute or rule to be incompatible with Community law. Instead, the European Court considers itself able to provide the national court with all matters relating to the interpretation of Community law as may enable it to decide the issue of compatibility in the case before it; see *Schumacher* v *Hauptzollamt Frankfurt Am Main* (7).

In the event of a conflict, the Court may only conclude that the relevant provisions of national law appear 'incompatible' with Community law. It is the responsibility of the national court to ensure that the relevant Community law is applied and to determine whether a plaintiff, the prosecution or the defence should prevail.

If a national court decides not to make a preliminary reference to the European Court, then the other situation when a conflict will arise is when the national court or tribunal is required to rule on the point.

Resolution of the conflict in the view of the ECJ

According to the European Court, conflicts between Community law and provisions of national law should always be resolved in favour of the Community rules. In one of its earliest decision, the Court declared:

> '[T]he law stemming from the Treaty, an independent source of law, cannot, because of its special and original nature, be overridden by domestic legal provisions, however framed, without being deprived

of its character as Community law and without the legal basis of the Community itself being called into question'; *Costa* v *ENEL* (8).

Community law therefore prevails over inconsistent provisions of national law whether enacted before or after the Community Treaties entered into force. Further, as formulated by the Court, the principle of supremacy must also be given effect within the national legal systems of the Member States.

The Court has consistently maintained this principle throughout the course of its jurisprudence. For example, most recently, the European Court was asked by the House of Lords for a ruling on whether that court was required to grant interim relief in a case in which provisions of the Merchant Shipping Act 1988 were challenged as being incompatible with Community law.

In its decision, the European Court held that 'any legislative, administrative or judicial practice' which might impair the effectiveness of Community law is incompatible with Community law and cannot be applied by a national court. Hence, a national court which would normally grant interim relief in such circumstances, if it were not for a rule of national law to the contrary, is required 'to set aside that rule'; *R* v *Secretary of State, ex parte Factortame* (9).

In is therefore clear that the European Court will not entertain the prospect of any provision of national law, even of constitutional validity, prevailing over an inconsistent provision of Community law. Hence, this is one of the most vigorously asserted principles formulated by the European Court and there are no circumstances to date in which a conflict between a Community rule and a national rule has been resolved in favour of the national rule.

References

(1) [1989] 2 WLR 997
(2) [1979] ECR 1629
(3) [1989] 2 CMLR 751
(4) [1974] ECR 837
(5) [1970] ECR 1125
(6) [1985] 2 CMLR 259
(7) [1990] 2 CMLR 465
(8) [1964] ECR 585
(9) [1990] 3 CMLR 867

QUESTION 4

General Comment

A very popular question with examiners. The quotation from the Advocate-General embodies the limitations of the principle of the direct effect of directives. The question tests knowledge of the application of this principle and how far the European Court is prepared to extend the principle to give private individuals rights against other private individuals with regard to unimplemented directives. The answer must, however, take into account the recent jurisprudence of the European Court.

Skeleton Solution

The distinction between the relative legal qualities of directives and regulations.

The principles behind the direct effect of unimplemented directives.

The distinction between horizontal and vertical direct effect.

The limitations imposed on the principle by the ECJ.

The judgments of the Court in *Von Colson* and *Marleasing*.

Suggested Solution

The two main instruments of Community legislation are regulations and directives. Under Article 189 of the EC Treaty, regulations are 'binding in their entirety and directly applicable in all Member States'. In contrast, directives, while also binding as far as the object to be achieved, are not directly applicable and national authorities are permitted to select the appropriate forms and methods of implementation. While Community regulations, once enacted, automatically create rights and obligations, according to the strict terms of the EC Treaty, Community directives do not create any such rights or obligations until implemented by Member States.

Regulations and directives are employed at the Community level for different purposes. Regulations are designed as measures permitting the Community institutions to legislate directly throughout the whole of the Community. Directives are most often used when legal standards are being harmonised throughout the Community but these standards need not be identical in each Member State as long as a minimum level of protection is provided.

The most significant distinction between the two types of legislation is that private individuals and legal persons may rely on the terms of a Community regulation to establish rights without the need for intervention on the part of a legislative organ such as the British Parliament. Community regulations may form grounds of action or establish defences for private individuals. Such rights are directly applicable and hence directly enforceable before national courts and tribunals.

True, occasionally Community regulations are re-enacted in national legislative provisions to provide greater clarity or to create penalties for failure to comply with the terms of the regulation. However, in such cases the force of law continues to reside in the regulation and is not superseded by the national measure. In the event of a conflict between the regulation and the national measure, the Community regulation prevails.

Regulations are therefore the most effective and comprehensive form of legislation that may be adopted by Community institutions. Directives, on the other hand, are less comprehensive in their coverage than regulations and also lack the automatic effect possessed by regulations.

This is the position as strictly delineated in Article 189 of the EC Treaty. However, this distinction is no longer clear-cut. The European Court has developed the principle of the direct effect of directives to allow private individuals to rely on the terms of unimplemented directives if certain conditions have been satisfied. The principle has been developed in response to the failure of Member States to timeously implement directives which has the effect of frustrating the purposes of the measures and denying individuals private rights.

The European Court has been prepare to give 'vertical direct effect' to directives which have remained unimplemented by Member States after the period provided for the adoption of the measure into national law. In other words, the Court has been prepared to refuse to allow the failure of a state to adopt a directive as a justification for denying private individuals their legitimate rights.

But the right to rely on the terms of an unimplemented directive is not absolute. Three conditions must be satisfied before reliance can be placed on the measure. First, the terms of the directive must be sufficiently precise to allow the creation of directly enforceable legal obligations. Second, the provision must specify an obligation which is not subject to any qualification, exception or condition. Third, the provision must not require intervention on the part of a Community institution or a Member State. These are the necessary pre-requisites for a directive to be considered as having direct effect.

There are, however, two major limitations placed on the application of the principle of direct effect itself.

Firstly, the principle applies only to directives which remain unimplemented after the date has passed for adoption. The entry into force of directives which have been adopted, but which have not yet entered into force, cannot be anticipated or pre-empted.

Secondly, and more importantly, the Court has only been prepared to apply this principle to the relationships between individuals and the national authorities as opposed to the relationships among private individuals themselves. In other words, while an individual can invoke an unimplemented directive against national authorities, the rights conferred by the unimplemented directives cannot be enforced in private relationships.

The application of the principle of direct effect to private relationships is known as 'horizontal direct effect' as opposed to 'vertical direct effect' which refers to the relationship between individuals and the state. In fact, it was in the case cited in the question, *Marshall* v *Southampton and South-West Hampshire Area Health Authority* (1), that the European Court denied that unimplemented directives were capable of horizontal direct effect. As we can see, the Advocate-General suggested to the Court that this approach should be adopted.

But in fact although the principle of horizontal direct effect is beyond the purview of the European Court, the Court has given a broad interpretation to the national authorities and agencies against whom unimplemented directives may be enforced. Unimplemented directives have been applied as a defence to a prosecution by public authorities (*Pubblico Ministero* v *Ratti* (2)), against tax authorities (*Becker* v *Finanzamt Munster-Innenstadt* (3)), against government departments (*Van Duyn* v *Home Office* (4)) and against local government bodies (*R* v *London Boroughs Transport Committee* (5)).

In addition, the principle applies to all bodies or organisations which are subject to the control of the state or which possess special powers beyond those which result from the normal rules applicable to relations between individuals; see *Foster & Others* v *British Gas Plc* (6). Crown bodies, authorities responsible for the maintenance of public order and safety and public corporations are all emanations of the state for the purpose of applying the principle of direct effect to unimplemented directives; see *Johnston* v *Chief Constable of the Royal Ulster Constabulary* (7).

That is not, however, the end of the matter. The situation has been made more complex by decisions of the Court which, while continuing the general policy of refusing to give horizontal direct effect to directives, have nevertheless opened an alternative channel to allow relief to private individuals denied their rights against other individuals because a Member State has failed to implement a directive in time.

First, in *Von Colson* v *Land Nordrhein-Westfahlen* (8), and more recently in *Marleasing SA* v *La Commercial Internacional De Alimentacion SA* (9), the Court has given indirect effect to unimplemented directives via Article 5 of the EC Treaty. This article requires Member States to 'take all appropriate measures' to ensure the fulfilment of the obligations arising out of the Treaty.

In the *Marleasing* case, the plaintiffs alleged that a Spanish company had been wound up for the purpose of defrauding its creditors. The company was formed by a founders contract which is an agreement among the participants in the company to establish the company. This is a legitimate means of incorporating a company under Spanish law. The plaintiffs were challenging the winding-up on the basis that the founders contract was void for lack of consideration, also a concept recognised in Spanish company law. If the contract was void, the directors would be liable for its debt since there would have been no valid incorporation in the first place.

The grounds on which a company can be annulled are exhaustively listed in Council Directive 68/151. Lack of consideration is not one of the grounds listed in the directive but in any event the Spanish government had not implemented its terms at the time the dispute arose. The defendants relied on this directive to support the assertion that the company could not be wound up for lack of consideration because this was not a ground for declaring a company void under the directive. The Court was asked to rule on the effect of the unimplemented directive on the relationship between these two private parties.

While the Court rejected the notion of horizontal direct effect, it observed that Article 5 of the EC Treaty placed Member States under an obligation to give effect to Community obligations. Spanish law had to be interpreted in light of this obligation. Hence, Spanish company law was to be interpreted and applied in terms compatible with the directive. Since the directive exhaustively listed all the grounds for annulling a company, the Spanish company could not be annulled for lack of consideration. Hence the directors were not personally liable for the debts of the company.

It is difficult to avoid the conclusion that this decision was simply a means of permitting horizontal direct effect through interpretative sleight of hand. In other words, the Court is prepared to apply the terms of unimplemented directives to the relationships between individuals where this can be achieved by means of interpretative implication.

But even the development of this principle does not end the distinction between regulations and directives. Nevertheless, at the moment the actual effects and impact of the Court's decisions are not clear and will require further elaboration from the Court itself.

However, Advocate-General Slynn's convictions that allowing horizontal direct effect to directives would blur the distinction between the two types of measures does appear to be an exaggeration of the position since the Court is applying unimplemented directives by interpretative means without any great difficulty.

References

(1) [1986] ECR 723
(2) [1979] ECR 1629
(3) [1982] ECR 53
(4) [1974] ECR 1337
(5) [1990] 1 CMLR 229
(6) [1990] 2 CMLR 833
(7) [1986] ECR 1651
(8) [1984] ECR 1891
(9) [1992] 1 CMLR 305

QUESTION 5

General Comment

This is a problem-type question requiring the application of the relevant law to the hypothetical facts presented. The necessary figures are provided to establish the position of the hypothetical company on the market and the facts stated evidence abuse. However, exactly what the examiner requires by way of an answer is not well stated.

Skeleton Solution

Outline of the requirements for establishing an infringement of Article 86: dominant position, abuse, effect on trade between Member States

Establishing a dominant position: relevant product market, relevant geographical market, market share

Abusive behaviour: conditions and requirements

Penalties, sanctions, etc imposed by the Commission

Suggested Solution

a) Fruit Company should be advised that, should its activities amount to a dominant position within the Community for the production and sale of Peach Delight, then the two practices which it is presently engaged in – namely refusal to supply and excessive pricing – are likely to amount to an abuse of that position under Article 86 of the Treaty.

To assess whether the European Commission will find an abuse of a dominant position, it is necessary to calculate whether or not Fruit Ltd has a dominant position within the relevant market for its product and to apply the criteria used by the Commission and the Court to decide whether these two practices amount to an abuse.

Existence of a dominant position

The first step towards determining the existence of an abuse of a dominant position is to ascertain whether or not Fruit Delight possesses a dominant position in terms of Article 86. This requires examination of two factors: (i) identification of the relevant market; (ii) calculation of Fruit Delight's market share.

i) *Relevant market*

The relevant market is defined in terms of both the product market and the geographical market.

To identify the relevant product market it is necessary to isolate the product under investigation from similar products in the market-place. For this purpose, the relevant product includes the actual product under consideration together with all other products which may be substituted, in terms of production and use, for the actual product. In this particular case, the relevant product is therefore Peach Delight and all other fruits which can be considered substitutes.

The test for identifying substitutable products depends on whether or not there is'a sufficient degree of interchangeability' between all the products forming part of the same market; *Hoffmann-La-Roche & Co AG* v *EC Commission* (1). Where a product is interchangeable with the product under investigation, then that product too forms part of the relevant product market.

Whether another product is sufficiently interchangeable with the product under investigation, and hence part of the relevant product market, is measured by two factors. First, the objective physical characteristics of the product must be similar to the product under consideration, in this case Peach Delight. Second, the competitive conditions and the structure of the supply and demand for the product on the market must also be similar to those for Peach Delight.

For fresh fruit, the Court has already ruled that the important physical qualities which require consideration are the characteristics of the product gauged in terms of appearance, taste, softness and ease of handling; *United Brands* v *EC Commission* (2). So, it is possible that, on the basis of this test, both peaches and apricots will be included within the scope of the relevant market since the Peach Fruit in a hybrid of both of these. However, much will depend on the factual physical features of the Peach Delight.

As regards competitive conditions, the Court, in the *United Brands* case, supra, considered four factors to be germane in identifying interchangeable products in terms of this condition, namely;

- the degree to which the principal product is affected by falling or increasing prices of other fruits;

- the purchasing habits of consumers relative to expenditure on the principal product compared to other types of fresh fruit;
- the existence of special purchasing groups such as sectors of the community which consider the principal product to be a necessary dietary requirement; and
- growing season for the particular product relative to other fruits.

So, if other fruits share similar pricing patterns, purchasing habits of consumers, and the growing seasons of the Peach Delight, they will be considered relevant products in the event that their physical characteristics are also sufficiently similar.

In these circumstances, it is likely that peaches and apricots will also be included in the relevant product market along with Peach Delight since products which are produced by means of cross-fertilisation generally share some features in common with the products from which they have been produced.

The relevant geographical market is considerably more easy to ascertain. The relevant geographical market is defined as the area within the Community 'where the conditions are sufficiently homogeneous for the effect of economic power of the undertaking concerned to be evaluated'; *United Brands*, supra. The geographical market will be the whole Community unless there are factual reasons for limiting the area to a lesser size while still satisfying the criterion of being 'a substantial part' of the Community.

Factors generally relied on to limit the geographical scope of the relevant geographical market include impediments to cross-border trade such as physical, technological, legal or cultural barriers to trade, the lack of adequate transportation facilities, or the inability to extend distribution or supply networks into certain regions.

The facts presented in the question state that Fruit Limited has a 48 per cent share of the total Peach Delight market in the Community and is the sole Community supplier. Hence, there is no reason for believing that factors limiting the scope of the geographical market exist and the geographical market is therefore the whole of the Community.

Applying both the tests for the relevant product market and the relevant geographical market to the facts stated in the question, the relevant market is therefore probably the market throughout the Community for Peach Delight, apricots and peaches.

ii) *Market share*

We are informed that Fruit Limited has a market share of 48 per cent in the total Peach Delight market in the Community and a 5 per cent share of the market for fresh fruit. Since it is the sole Community producer for Peach Delight, the remaining market share in that product must be imported from non-Community producers.

Since the relevant product market will most likely include peaches and apricots, the market share held by Fruit Delight in the relevant product market will be less than 48 per cent and higher than 5 per cent. The exact share will have to be calculated in light of the statistics for the markets in apricots and peaches.

Naturally the market share held by Fruit Ltd is the critical factor in establishing whether or not it possesses a dominant position. But no absolute percentage share of the relevant market has ever been considered by the Court or the Commission to definitively establish the existence of a dominant position. Thus, in the *United Brands* case, above, a market share of 40 per cent was considered sufficient to establish dominance. However, the Commission has in the past taken the view that a market share of 20–40 per cent of the relevant market may constitute dominance if certain circumstances are shown to exist.

Hence, it is more likely than not that Peach Delight will be considered to have a dominant position in the market.

Existence of an abuse of position

Abuse of a position is an objective concept which relates to the behaviour of the company under investigation. Article 86 itself identifies some of the practices which may be considered abuse. These include directly or indirectly imposing unfair purchase or selling prices or other unfair trading conditions.

Fruit Limited is possibly guilty of two forms of abusive practices: refusing to supply purchasers with Peach Delight unless they agree to sell no other soft fruits; and charging excessive prices relative to production costs.

Fruit Ltd's refusal to supply is a flagrant abuse of its dominant position. Companies and producers cannot use their positions within particular markets to impose their unreasonable terms and conditions of sale on customers.

Dominant companies may only refuse to supply customers where there is an objectively justifiable reason for such a refusal. Where an order is made in the ordinary course of trade and can be easily satisfied, a dominant company cannot flex its economic muscle to impose unfair terms on customers; see *Hilti* v *EC Commission* (3).

Fruit Ltd is also guilty of abusing its dominant position by charging excessive prices. Prices are excessive if they bear no 'reasonable relation to the economic value of the product supplied'; *General Motors* v *EC Commission* (4). The test of excess pricing involves a comparison between the selling price of the product and the costs of production, thereby disclosing the margin of profit.

Fruit Ltd makes each Peach Delight at a cost of 5p, including both cultivation and production costs. Even once distribution costs, marketing expenditure, commissions, etc, are deducted Fruit Ltd cannot justify the profit margin which results after charging 75p for each fruit. Therefore, it is likely that they have also abused their dominant position by engaging in excessive pricing.

Consequences of a determination of abuse of position

It is extremely likely that the Commission will find Fruit Ltd guilty of an abuse of a dominant position. This will result in two immediate consequences. First, the Commission is empowered to impose fines and second the Commission can issue a cease and desist order to compel Fruit Ltd to discontinue its present conditions of sale policy.

The Commission is authorised to impose fines up to ECU 1,000,000 or, alternatively, a sum in excess of these limits but not exceeding 10 percent of the annual turnover of a company found to have violated Article 86. The Commission assesses the quantum of fine according to the nature of the anti-competitive practices found to exist, the duration of the practices and the market position of the company infringing the Article.

In this particular case, Fruit Ltd must be advised that a heavy fine can be expected, specifically because of the nature of its anti-competitive practices. It should therefore immediately engage in a damage limitation exercise by introducing a competition compliance programme, revise its terms and conditions of sale to remove both abusive practices and assist the Commission to the greatest extent possible throughout the course of its investigation.

b) In theory at least, Mr Robinson can rely on the terms of both Articles 85 and 86 of the EC Treaty. Article 85 prohibits anti-competitive agreements contravening its terms while Article 86 prohibits companies and undertakings abusing their dominant positions. These articles are not mutually exclusive and it is perfectly possible that a particular practice may infringe both provisions; see *In Re Italian Flat Glass Suppliers* (5).

If Mr Robinson wishes to rely on Article 85(1) he must establish that there exists an agreement between himself and Fruit Limited. Thus, for example, if an agreement previously existed according to which Mr Robinson agreed to Fruit Ltd's conditions of sale, and this was terminated because Mr Robinson refused to comply with these terms, Article 85(1) would probably apply.

However, he would be on more solid ground under Article 86 of the EC Treaty. As noted above, Fruit Ltd are in flagrant violation of the obligation contained in that provision not to engage in an abuse of its dominant position. The abuse in question has had a direct effect on the trading activities of Mr Robinson and it is likely that he would be able to establish injury, in particular by the refusal to sell unless the unfair trading conditions are accepted.

Mr Robinson has two separate remedies available. First, he can complain to the European Commission that Fruit Ltd is abusing its dominant position. Such a complaint has a number of advantages. The Commission would assume responsibility for pursuing the matter should it decide that the complaint is valid. Hence, Mr Robinson would incur nominal expenses by proceeding in this manner.

On the other hand, he cannot compel the Commission to pursue the complaint and, even if the Commission brought the matter to a successful conclusion, he would not be automatically entitled to compensation for injury suffered as a result of the anti-competitive practice.

The alternative course of action is to raise proceedings in the English courts directly against Fruit Ltd. First, an application for an interlocutory injunction to restrain the refusal to supply can be made by a plaintiff; see *Garden Cottage Foods* v *Milk Marketing Board* (6).

Second, an action for damages for injury caused can be commenced on the ground of breach of statutory duty against Fruit Ltd on the basis of injury suffered to Mr Robinson's business by the refusal to supply; see *Commission Notice on Co-operation with National Courts in the Enforcement of Community*

Competition Law 1993. This would probably provide the best relief to Mr Robinson against the abuses being perpetrated by Fruit Ltd.

References

(1) [1979] ECR 461
(2) [1978] ECR 207
(3) [1992] 4 CMLR 16
(4) [1975] ECR 1367
(5) [1992] 5 CMLR 302
(6) [1983] 3 WLR 143

QUESTION 6

General Comment

This is a three-part question concerning the application of Articles 30 and 36 of the EC Treaty with the exception of part (a) which requires consideration of the concept of charges having an equivalent effect to customs duties. The issues raised are relatively novel and require a moment of reflection prior to answering the question properly.

Skeleton Solution

a) The terms of Article 30, de facto discrimination and the exceptions contained in Article 36.

   Article 12 and the principle of charges having an equivalent effect.

b) The *Cassis de Dijon Case* and the principle of mandatory requirements.

   The requirements of non-discrimination and proportionality.

c) The principles behind the ECJ decision in *Stoke-on-Trent* v *B & Q plc.*

   Concept of socio-economic function and the requirements on non-discrimination and proportionality.

Suggested Solution

a) A distinction must be drawn between the financial levy imposed on the books published within a Member State and the levy or charge imposed on the importation of foreign language books into the Member State.

   Article 30 of the EC Treaty prohibits quantitative restrictions and measures having equivalent effects to quantitative restrictions. Measures having an equivalent effect have been defined by the European Court as 'all trading rules enacted by Member States which are capable of hindering, directly or indirectly, actually or potentially, intra-Community trade'; *Procureur du Roi* v *Dassonville* (1).

   Quite clearly the legislation imposing a financial levy on

books published within the Member State would fall into this category if it in some way limited the sale of foreign language books within the country. While prima facie the financial levy applies to both national and foreign publishers of foreign-language books, in practice this measure amounts to discrimination because its impact will be felt disproportionately by foreign producers. Few publishers within the Member State will be engaged in the publication of foreign language books in comparison to producers in other Member States who will mainly produce publications in their own langauge.

Hence, although the measure is not discriminatory on the face of it, in effect it will cause discrimination by burdening foreign producers with higher costs than those incurred by national producers publishing in their own language. This is an example of de facto discrimination as opposed to de jure discrimination.

By causing discrimination between national and non-national producers, the legislation constitutes a measure which hinders trade between Member States and which therefore constitutes a measure having an effect equivalent to a quantitative restriction contrary to Article 30.

The Member State cannot rely on the terms of Article 36, which contain the exceptions to the general principle prohibiting measures having an equivalent effect to quantitative restrictions. The law cannot be justified on the basis of an attempt to protect public morality, public policy, the protection of national heritage or to protect industrial or commercial property.

In particular, the exception relating to the protection of national heritage does not extend to linguistic protection and in any event it is unlikely that this objective would be secured by the imposition of a financial levy.

In addition to violating Article 30, it is also likely that the financial levy imposed on the importation of foreign language books infringes Article 12 of the EC Treaty. This provision prohibits all charges having an equivalent effect to customs duties. These are defined as 'any pecuniary charge, whatever its designation and mode of application, which is imposed unilaterally on goods by reason of the fact that they cross a frontier'; *EC Commission* v *Germany* (*Re Customs Inspection Fees*) (2).

If the legislation imposes a charge on the importation of the foreign language books when they cross the frontiers into the Member State, this will involve a violation of Article 12 unless the charge relates to a general system of internal dues applied systematically within a Member State without discrimination between domestic and imported products; *Denkavit* v *France* (3).

Clearly in this case the pecuniary charge is not non-discriminatory even although it applies to both national publishers and foreign publishers quite simply because it causes de facto discrimination.

b) The legislation of the Member State requiring all novels sold in the country to state on the title page the nationality of the author also requires scrutiny under Article 30 to verify whether or not it amounts to a measure having an equivalent effect to a quantitative restriction.

This requirement will violate Article 30 if it amounts to a rule capable of hindering intra-Community trade. In essence, the measure amounts to a marketing requirement and it is well settled in the jurisprudence of the European Court that obstacles to movement of goods within the Community resulting from national laws relating to the marketing of products are acceptable if they are required to satisfy 'mandatory requirements' relating in particular to the protection of public health, the fairness of commercial transactions and the defence of the consumer; see *Cassis de Dijon Case* (4).

In other words, the Member State would have to demonstrate that the requirement was necessary to ensure the fairness of commercial transactions or to protect consumers from unfair trade practices. It is unlikely that the Member State would be successful in establishing that either of these conditions was applicable. The requirement does not serve a purpose which could be said to be in the general interests of the public and the objective of the measure is not of sufficient magnitude to take precedence over the obligation of Member States to ensure the free movement of goods.

Any such mandatory requirement must remain proportionate to the objective sought to be achieved and cannot cause discrimination between foreign and domestic goods. It is unlikely that either of these conditions is satisfied by the legislation requiring novels to state the nationality of the author. If anything, the requirement is an attempt to indulge in de facto discrimination by encouraging consumers to purchase books written by authors from Member States. There can be few other reasons for the introduction of such a measure.

c) This legislation must also be assessed against the obligations contained in Article 30. It the *Cassis de Dijon Case*, supra, the

European Court first hinted that Article 30 could apply to measures within a Member State regulating the production and marketing of a product without any overt manifestation of discrimination between domestic and imported goods.

The Court held that, in the absence of Community rules relating to the production and marketing of alcohol products, it was for the Member States themselves to regulate all matters relating to the production and marketing of alcohol and alcoholic beverages within their territories. Further, it was a legitimate purpose of such regulations to protect the health of the consumer.

Only if the mandatory requirements imposed on the production and marketing of the products were disproportionate to the object sought to be achieved, or amounted to discrimination, is there a violation of the terms of Article 30.

The legislation presumably is based on the need to protect the public from the dangers of alcohol abuse and therefore has a legitimate aim. Allowing individuals to manufacture alcohol in their own private households is consistent with this objective since the overall impact of the measure would be to dramatically reduce alcohol consumption throughout the population.

The measure also affects the sale of both domestic and imported products equally and does not create any overt form of discrimination in favour of national products. The marketing of the alcoholic drinks is not made more difficult than the marketing of national products.

In addition, there is a solid argument that the measure is not disproportionate to the objective sought to be achieved, namely a reduction in the amount of alcohol consumed by the population. The protection of the public from alcohol abuse may justifiably warrant such measures. In assessing the proportionality requirement it is also necessary to weigh the national interest in attaining that aim against the Community interest in ensuring the free movement of goods.

National rules restricting the sale of alcohol therefore pursue an aim which is justified under Community law. These rules reflect choices relating to particular national socio-cultural characteristics. It is therefore for the Member States to select the proper means of regulating alcohol consumption in compliance with the requirements of Community law and in particular the principle of proportionality; see *Stoke-on-Trent City Council* v *B & Q plc* (5).

References

(1) [1974] ECR 837
(2) [1990] 1 CMLR 561
(3) [1979] ECR 1923
(4) [1979] ECR 649
(5) [1993] 1 CMLR 426

QUESTION 7

General Comment

Two separate issues are raised in this question. The first is the right of a Community national to seek employment in another Member States which involves the application of Article 48 and the related secondary legislation. The second is the issue of equal pay for part-time workers which is an Article 119 issue. In this connection, there is also recent caselaw from the ECJ with which the student must be familiar in order to respond properly.

Skeleton Solution

Free movement of persons: Article 48 and Regulation 1612/68.

Eligibility and equality in employment.

Article 48(4) exception: employment in the public sector.

Equal pay: Article 119 and the ECJ in the *Nimz* case.

Suggested Solution

Article 48 of the EC Treaty establishes the right of Community workers to travel from their own country to another Member State for the purposes of seeking and accepting offers of employment. Community workers are also entitled, by virtue of the same provision, to reside in that Member State to exercise the right to work and to remain in the territory of the Member State after having been employed there. These basic rights have been supplemented by a considerable volume of supporting secondary legislation.

The rights bestowed by Community law under the freedom of movement of workers are conferred only on those individuals who qualify as 'workers' in terms of Article 48. A worker is a person engaged in a contract of employment which will be the case should Kirsten accept the terms of the contract presently being offered to her by Verona City Council. It is irrelevant for the purposes of Community law that the contract is part-time. As the Court has pointed out a person who is employed on a part-time basis may acquire the right of freedom of movement provided that he or she pursues an activity as an employed person which is 'effective and genuine'; see *Levin* v *Staatssecretaris van Justitie* (1).

One of the fundamental rights conferred by the principle of the free movement of workers is that all discrimination based on nationality as regards the conditions of employment, remuneration and other conditions, is to be abolished by virtue of Article 48(2) of the EC Treaty. This obligation has been given effect in secondary legislation by Council Regulation 1612/68 (1968).

According to Article 1 of this Regulation, workers are entitled to take up employment in the territory of a Member State with the same priority as nationals of that state. Employment contracts must be issued in accordance with the provisions of the law in force and, in particular, without any discrimination. National provisions are expressly declared inapplicable when they limit the rights of workers to take up and pursue employment.

These rights are, however, subject to the overriding exception stated in Article 48(4) which expressly declares that the obligation of non-discrimination on the grounds of nationality does not apply to employment in the public service. However, this exception is not as general as might first be believed.

First, the proviso does not apply to all types of employment in the public sector. In *EC Commission* v *Belgium* (2), the European Court found that the Article applied only to those posts which required direct or indirect involvement in exercising powers 'conferred by public law and duties designed to safeguard the general interests of the state and other public authorities'. These posts normally involve some form of allegiance to the state.

Hence, the Court cited a range of positions which fell outside this exception including train drivers, plumbers and nurses. On the other hand, works supervisors and office supervisors were considered as falling within the exception since they involved safeguarding the interests of the state.

The job that has been offered to Kirsten is that of a civil engineer with Verona City Council. The factors which operate against any assumption that this is a post which falls within Article 48(4) are that there is no particular element of allegiance to the state required of a civil engineer and that her position is a minor one with no supervisory functions or responsibilities. It is therefore more than likely that the position does not fall within Article 48(4) and that the exception contained therein is inapplicable.

It should also be noted that once Kirsten has been accepted for the position, no discrimination on the grounds of nationality may be perpetrated in terms of the conditions of employment applicable once appointed; see *Sotgiu* v *Deutsche Bundespost* (3). Kirsten would therefore be well-advised to accept the terms of her offer, ignore her lawyer's advice, and rely on her Community rights under the freedom of movement of persons once appointed.

Kirsten may rely on a different set of Community rights in order to challenge the gender discrimination encountered in her conditions of employment. Article 119 of the EC Treaty sets out these rights and basically provides that both genders must receive 'equal pay for equal work'. This provision has been given direct effect in a whole host of cases; see for example *Defrenne* v *Sabena* (4). This basic provision has also been supplemented by considerable secondary legislation, mainly in the form of directives.

In order to be successful, Kirsten will have to establish that two conditions exist. First, that she is not receiving equal pay, as defined in Community law, for equal work. Second, that the discrimination is based on a distinction between genders.

'Equal pay' is defined in Article 119 as 'the ordinary basic or minimum wage or salary and any other consideration, whether in cash or kind, which the worker received, directly or indirectly, in respect of his [or her] employment from his [or her] employer'. The European Court has defined 'pay' in very broad terms indeed. Thus, special allowances, discriminatory retirement periods, pension allowances and redundancy payments, all constitute pay within the meaning of the Article.

Quite clearly, the fact that she is to be paid at a lesser rate than full time male colleagues doing essentially the same job amounts to discrimination unless there are objective criteria on which such discrimination may legitimately be based. Similarly, the fact that female employees are required to retire prior to the dates set for their male counterparts has, for some considerable period, been considered contrary to the equal pay for equal work principle; see for example, *Marshall* v *Southampton and South-West Hampshire Area Health Authority (No 1)* (5); *Barber* v *Guardian Royal Exchange Assurance Group* (6).

One defence which might be offered by Verona City Council is that, because Kirsten will be employed on a part-time basis, and her male counterparts work on a full-time basis, then Kirsten is not doing equal work to that of her male colleagues. The European Court has recently considered this issue in *Nimz* v *Freie Und Hansestadt Hamburg* (7). In this case, the plaintiff was a part-time worker paid at a lesser rate than her full-time male colleagues. The question asked of the European Court on a preliminary reference was whether both sets of employees were engaged in equal work in terms of Article 119.

The Court held that whether part-time and full-time work in the same general role amounted to equal work under Article 119 was to be determined on the basis of objective criteria which are unrelated to any discrimination on the ground of gender. In this context, the amount of experience acquired by a full-time employee in relation to that acquired by a part-time employee was significant insofar as the full-time employee can more quickly gain experience. Whether or not this is the case depends on the relationship between the nature of the work performed and the experience gained from the performance of that work on completion of a certain amount of working hours.

In practical terms, the Court's decision is in essence a statement that the more complex, the more skilled and the less repetitive or mundane the work involved in the position, the more likely that a distinction between part-time workers and full-time workers will be justified on the basis that the two positions do not involve similar work. Other factors which will support the argument that, despite the part-time/full-time distinction, both are engaged in equal work, include the same hourly rates of pay, the same degree of job responsibility and the same job description.

Kirsten must also establish that the discrimination is based on gender. As regards her pay her case will be assisted if she can demonstrate that an overwhelming proportion of full-time employees are male while the majority of part-time employees are female. Her case would also be reinforced if she could demonstrate that part-time male colleagues were being paid at the same rate as their full-time counterparts. On the other hand, if the majority of part-time workers are male, and if they are paid at the same rate as Kirsten, the onus would be on Kirsten to demonstrate that there is still discrimination.

The requirement that female employees must retire at 55 while their male colleagues are permitted to work until the age of 60 is a clear-cut violation of Article 119. The retirement requirement applies regardless of the nexus between the gender of the employee and the particular position which is involved. There is an across-the-board policy that male employees retire at 60 and female employees at 55 regardless of job responsibilities and positions. Policies such as these have, for some considerable period, been considered to violate Article 119; see *Defrenne*, supra.

References

(1) [1982] ECR 1035
(2) [1980] ECR 3881
(3) [1974] ECR 307

References (continued)
(4) [1976] 2 CMLR 98
(5) [1986] ECR 723
(6) [1990] CMLR 513
(7) [1992] 3 CMLR 699

QUESTION 8

General Comment

This is an essay-type question requiring a narrative answer and concerns the recent constitutional developments within the Community. In order to answer the question properly, it is necessary to be familiar with the background to the changes and to offer a well-reasoned legal opinion on the effects that the changes will bring.

Skeleton Solution

The problems encountered in the operation of the original Article 171: repetitive actions, non-implementation, delay.

Outline of the terms of new Article 171(2).

Shortcomings of the amendments: uncertainty, mechanisms for enforcement.

Decision of the ECJ in the *Francovich* case and the conditions for establishing liability.

Contribution of these changes to enforcement of Community law in Member States by the Commission *and* private individuals.

Suggested Solution

The original terms of Article 171 of the EC Treaty merely required Member States found in violation of their Community obligations by the European Court to 'take the necessary measures' to comply with the judgment. No other mechanism was created to enforce judgments against Member States. Nor were any sanctions specified for failure to comply with the terms of an adverse decision.

On the whole, this obligation was sufficient to compel most Member States to amend their laws to comply with the decisions of the Court. However, certain states, in particular Italy, acquired a reputation for ignoring the rulings of the Court. Other states, such as France, refused to obey the decisions of the Court when it ruled against them on particularly sensitive issues. While the record for complying with the decisions of the Court was initially respectable, towards the end of the early 1980s, the position had deteriorated and in 1991 the European Commission reported that over 50 decisions of the Court remained unimplemented.

There are a number of notorious cases where Member States persistently refused to adhere to the decisions of the Court. For example, in 1969 the European Court ruled that an Italian law imposing an export tax on art treasures was contrary to the principle of the free movement of goods; *EC Commission* v *Italy (Re Tax on Art Treasures)* (1). Italy refused to amend its laws and a subsequent action was brought by the Commission; *EC Commission* v *Italy (Re Failure to Implement Community Obligations)* (2). Again Italy ignored the ruling and the matter was only eventually served through a political compromise.

Another illustration of a Member State refusing to comply with the decisions of the Court occurred when the Court condemned France for its ban on imports of mutton and lamb from the United Kingdom; *EC Commission v France (Re Imports of Mutton and Lamb)* (3). Again the Commission was required to bring fresh proceedings against France for violation of Articles 171 and 5 of the EC Treaty.

The increasing willingness of Member States to resist the rulings of the Court has been caused by two primary factors. First, although the Court has powers to grant interim measures in an action by the Commission for enforcement of a Court judgment under Article 186, it has been reluctant to use them to compel a Member State to comply with a ruling. For example, when France imposed the embargo on mutton and lamb products from the United Kingdom, the Court refused to grant the interim measures requested by the Commission because France was already under an obligation to implement the ruling by virtue of Article 171.

Second, Member States have traditionally been allowed a lengthy period to comply with adverse rulings from the Court. Technically this period is restricted to the minimum period needed for the adoption of the necessary remedial measures; *EC Commission* v *France (Re Tobacco Prices)* (4). In practice, the workloads of the Commission and the Court, combined with the procrastinations of governments, mean that a Member State found in violation has an excessive period within which to act and most do act after a sufficient period. However, the effect of this situation is that there are lengthy delays pending the adoption of amending national laws.

In terms of the original Article 171, the only remedy available to the Commission to enforce a Court ruling was to repeatedly bring proceedings against Member States alleging that, in addition to the original violation, the states had also breached Article 171 by failing to implement the decision. Clearly this was an unsatisfactory situation.

The Treaty on European Union adds an additional paragraph to Article 171 and introduces a process whereby a Member State can be fined for failing to implement a Court ruling. This involves a three stage process.

Once a decision has been given by the Court and a Member State has not complied with its terms within a reasonable period, the Commission shall deliver a reasoned opinion to the state concerned after having given that state an opportunity to submit its observations on the matter. The reasoned opinion shall specify the points on which, in the opinion of the Commission, the Member State is not complying with the Court's decision.

The second stage involves a second action against the Member State, this time under Article 171(2) itself. In these proceedings, the Commission may specify any penalty which should be paid by the Member State for the failure to act. This penalty may take the form of either a lump sum or a penalty payment, the latter being a sum required to be paid by the Member State at regular intervals until the breach is remedied.

The final stage is for the Court to rule on the issue of whether the Member State has failed to comply with its obligations under Article 171(1). If it has not, the Court may require the Member State to pay the lump sum or penalty payment.

There is some scepticism as to how this procedure will work in practice and the extent to which this will resolve the problems surrounding the enforcement of Community law against Member States.

First, private individuals cannot raise actions in the European Court against Member States. Accordingly, this is not an avenue open to private individuals, only the European Commission. Private individuals must continue to rely on the remedies available in their national courts against government bodies alleged to have engaged in practices contrary to Community law.

Second, the exact powers of the Commission to specify the amount of the fine are not stated. There is no maximum, or minimum, level of fine which may be proposed by the Commission. It is also not clear whether the European Court is bound to impose the exact fine suggested by the Commission in the event that a Member State is found to have violated this obligation. Can the Court modify the proposed amount in accordance with the terms of its second ruling?

Third, there is no mechanism in the Article to compel a Member State to pay the sum. For example, the penalty cannot expressly be deducted from its budgetary contributions. Therefore, in the event that a Member State persistently refuses to pay the prescribed penalties there is little that can be done to compel it to do so. This is a substantial flaw in the procedure.

Hence, the amendment to Article 171 may not be as successful in ensuring the enforcement of judgments against Member States as it might appear at first sight.

The European Court's ruling in the *Francovich* case (5) is, however, a completely different matter. This case established the principle that Member States can be liable to private individuals for failing to comply with Community law if the failure causes injury or damage to those individuals.

The facts of this case may be briefly stated as follows. The plaintiff raised an action in an Italian court claiming damages for loss of salary caused by the failure of the Italian government to establish a fund to pay redundancy payments in the event that an employee is made redundant through the insolvency of his or her employer. The duty to establish such a fund was imposed by a Community directive which Italy had failed to implement.

The Italian court referred the question to the European Court for a preliminary ruling. The European Court replied that, under Community law, states are liable to private individuals for failing to comply with Community law if three conditions are satisfied:

- the purpose of the Community measure which was not respected by the Member State was to create private rights for individuals;
- the nature and content of these rights must be identifiable from the terms of the measure; and
- there must exist a causal link between the failure by the Member State to comply with Community law and the injury sustained by the individual.

In the event that these conditions are fulfilled, the Member State is liable to remedy the consequence of any damage or injury suffered as a result of the denial of Community rights.

However, again there are a number of shortcomings in the operation of this right. Each Member State is responsible for adopting procedures to allow for the vindication of this right. Hence, within the United Kingdom, the national courts are responsible for ensuring that a mechanism exists to bring such actions against the UK government. As yet, the legal basis for such a claim in English law is uncertain; see *Bourgoin* v *Ministry of Agriculture, Fisheries and Food* (6).

In addition, there is no certainty as to the types of Community measures that may be relied on to establish such rights. In the *Francovich* case itself, the infringement of Community law was a failure to implement the terms of a directive. It is not automatically the case that violations of EC Treaty articles, regulations, decisions or general principles of Community law will also result in this form of liability. This is a matter which the Court has still to resolve.

Also, it is not clear from the case whether or not the European Court must have held the Member State in question in violation of Community law through a direct action under Article 169. In the *Francovich* case, the Court had already found Italy in breach of Community law in an earlier direct action brought by the Commission. It is not apparent from the decision if such a ruling is a prerequisite to a successful action in a national court.

Notwithstanding these shortcomings, the Court's decision in this case is a landmark case establishing that Member States can be liable to private individuals for failing to comply with Community law. Prior to the ruling, this liability had not been definitively established; see *Asteris AE* v *Greece* (7). The Court has still to elaborate on the exact scope of this right, but there is little doubt that the decision will encourage a rash of cases on this point which will hopefully clarify the position.

But, since the principle of Member State responsibility for violations of Community law can be asserted in national courts, which have powers to enforce their decisions, this is likely to be a more effective remedy for private individuals seeking redress for injury suffered than the mechanisms which are to be introduced by Article 171(2).

References

(1) [1985] ECR 42
(2) [1972] ECR 527
(3) [1979] ECR 2729
(4) [1990] 1 CMLR 49
(5) [1992] IRLR 84
(6) [1986] 1 CMLR 267
(7) [1990] 1 CMLR 575

